THIS LITTLE ART

T0381927

Kate Briggs grew up in Somerset, UK, and lives and works in Rotterdam, NL, where she founded and co-runs the writing and publishing project 'Short Pieces That Move'. She is the translator of two volumes of Roland Barthes's lecture and seminar notes at the Collège de France: *The Preparation of the Novel* and *How to Live Together*, both published by Columbia University Press. In 2021, Kate Briggs was awarded a Windham-Campbell Prize. Her debut novel, *The Long Form*, was published by Fitzcarraldo Editions in 2023 and shortlisted for the Goldsmiths Prize the same year.

'Kate Briggs's *This Little Art* shares some wonderful qualities with Barthes's own work – the wit, thoughtfulness, invitation to converse, and especially the attention to the ordinary and everyday in the context of meticulously examined theoretical and scholarly questions. This is a highly enjoyable read: informative and stimulating for anyone interested in translation, writing, language, and expression.'
—— Lydia Davis, author and translator of Marcel Proust, Gustave Flaubert and A. L. Snijders

'In *This Little Art*, a digressive, scholarly, absorbing 350-page essay, Kate Briggs roams across the vast terrain – practical, theoretical, historical, philosophical – of translation. Briggs's writing is erudite and assured, while maintaining a tone that is modest and speculative; this paradox encapsulates something of the essence of translation, which is always contingent (no translation is ever definitive) yet also – for its time at least – authoritative.... There have been many books written about translation, but few as engaging, intriguing or exciting as Kate Briggs's exploration, with its digressive forays, infinite self-questioning, curiosity, modesty and devotion to the concrete – the very qualities, as it happens, that distinguish the translator's labour.'
—— Natasha Lehrer, *Times Literary Supplement*

'Maurice Blanchot once wrote that translators are "the silent masters of culture". Kate Briggs amends this, commenting that Blanchot wrote "hidden masters of culture" and that it's "our recognition" of translators' "zeal" that "remains silent".... Her engaging memoir unfolds in unnumbered, untitled, unstructured short chapters: a pillow book on the translator's love affair with words and writers.... Briggs can sound like a visionary.'
—— Marina Warner, *London Review of Books*

'*This Little Art* reads like a jubilant tribute to that vital impulse that marks the reader's attempt to engage with the pleasure of the text at the very basic level of language, a delight that derives from the minutiae of writing's unfolding, the joy of seeing both how contingent language is and yet how absolutely necessary it appears in the works of writers and their translators.... Briggs has written a testimony about the possibility of reading a text so intensely that one feels tempted to recreate it.'
—— Carlos Fonseca, *BOMB Magazine*

'*This Little Art* is generous, sentimental and needle-sharp, fierce and hesitant, flawed and perfect. All of it, all at once. This, in the end, is Briggs' dazzling conceit: *This Little Art* enacts what it is describing, the way it is written echoing what is written. We walk through her mind, we see her hover over thoughts, question herself, stop, start again. What could be read as misplaced self-effacement (Is this what I mean?, she wonders) is actually bold and brilliant: the gloriously digressive, curious, self-questioning, unapologetically subjective act of translation. In Briggs' pauses, negotiations, vacillations, queries and many varied answers we see a translator at work – a writer at work – deliberating, deciding, stopping the run, making art.'
—— Bella Bosworth, *Litro*

'Though it does not present itself as a memoir, a how-to guide, or a scholarly monograph, *This Little Art* derives its magic precisely from being all of these and more: gifting us not only with a genre-bending work of imaginative criticism, but also a fitting metaphor for all that the work of translation is, and can be.'
—— Theophilus Kwek, *Asymptote*

'Lucid and engaging, Briggs's book is essential, not just for translators, but anyone who has felt the magic of reading.'
—— *Publishers Weekly*, starred review

'*This Little Art* is a generous and wonderfully subversive re-orientation of a discourse often limited to notions of fidelity and failure, but also a celebration of translation's embeddedness in life.... The stories of two women translators endow the book with a passion and depth of character to rival a novel.'
— Madeleine LaRue, *Music & Literature*

'There is no other book on translation quite like *This Little Art*. It is a triumph and a joy; an ever-shifting kaleidoscope trained on a process which is too often invisible; and a reminder that choosing between one word and another is the basis not only of translation, but of working out what we think about the world.'
— *Review 31*

'*This Little Art* is rich, full of insightful anecdote and surprising analysis. But what sticks with me, what I have learned and retained from this teacher who was never my teacher, from this book that was never a textbook, is a vivid sense of how often the normal moves of translation critique miss almost everything that is worth noting about the "little art" they seek to elucidate, especially when they forget the importance of pace, when they disregard the fact that the writing-again that is translation is also a writing-anew, and when they ignore the motivations, affect, and singularity of individual translators.'
— Jan Steyn, *Music & Literature*

'Not so much a demystification as a re-enchantment of the practice of literary translation, that maddening, intoxicating "little" art which yokes humility and hubris, constraint and creativity – in Briggs's passionate telling, you can practically see the sparks fly.'
— Deborah Smith, translator of Han Kang and winner of the Man Booker International Prize in 2016

Fitzcarraldo Editions

THIS LITTLE ART

KATE BRIGGS

CONTENTS

DRAGONESE

It's Walpurgis-Nacht in the sanatorium and Hans Castorp, the hero of *The Magic Mountain*, has been made to feel hot and reckless by the atmosphere of carnival. Standing a small distance behind him, in the doorway of the little salon, is Frau Chauchat. She is dressed in a startling gown of thin, dark silk.

Was it black? Probably.

Or, at most, shot with golden brown.

Cut with a modest little neck, round like a school-girl's frock. Hardly so much as to show the base of her throat. Or the collar bones. Or, beneath the soft fringes of her hair, the slightly prominent bone at the back of her neck.

But all the while leaving bare to the shoulder her arms.

Arms so tender and so full.

So cool and so amazingly white, set off against the dark silk of her frock.

To such ravishing effect as to make Hans Castorp close his eyes. And murmur, deep within himself: 'O my God!'

He had once held a theory about those arms. He had thought, on making their acquaintance for the first time – veiled, as they had been then, in diaphanous gauze – that their indescribable, unreasonable seductiveness was down to the gauze itself. To the 'illusion', as he had called it. Folly! The utter, accentuated, blinding nudity of those arms was an experience now so intoxicating, compared with that earlier one, as to leave our man no other recourse than, once again, with drooping head, to whisper, soundlessly: 'O my God!'

Later, agitated by the silly drama of a drawing game, he'll walk straight up to her and boldly ask for a pencil.

She'll stand there, in her paper party cap, looking him up and down.

'I?' she'll ask. 'Perhaps I have, let me see.'

Eventually, she'll fetch one up from deep within her leather bag: a little silver one, slender and fragile, scarcely meant for use.

'*Voilà*,' she'll say, holding it up by its end in front of him, between thumb and forefinger, lightly turning it to and fro.

Because she won't quite hand it to him, because she'll give it to him and withhold it, he'll take it, so to speak, without receiving it: that is, he'll hold out his hand, ready to grasp the delicate thing, but without actually touching it.

'*C'est à visser, tu sais*,' she'll say. You have to unscrew it.

And with heads bent over it together, she'll show him the mechanism. It would be quite ordinary, the little needle of hard, probably worthless lead, coming down as one loosened the screw.

They'll stand bending toward each other. The stiff collar of his evening dress serving to support his chin.

She'll speak to him in French, and he'll follow her.

He'll speak to her in French uneasily, feeling for the sense.

A little further on she'll command, a bit exasperated and more impersonally now: '*Parlez allemand s'il vous plait!*'

And in the copy of the novel I have open next to me as I read and write, Hans Castorp replies in English. Clavdia Chauchat has asked him, pointedly, in French, to address her in German, and his reply is written for me in English. I mean, of course it is. It's an everyday peculiar thing: I am reading *The Magic Mountain* in Helen Lowe-Porter's translation, first published in 1927. A novel set high up in the Swiss Alps, one of Germany's most formative contributions to modern European literature (so the back cover of my edition tells me) and here they all are acting and interacting – not always, but for the most part – in English. And I go with it. I do. Of course I do. I willingly accept these terms. Positively and very gladly, in fact. Because with French but no German – I look at my bookshelves: also, no Italian and no Norwegian, no Japanese and no Spanish, no Danish and no Korean (and so on and so on) – I know that this is how the writing comes:

An unassuming young man named Hans Castorp travels up from his native city of Hamburg to Davos-Dorf. When the train stops at the small mountain station, he is surprised to hear his cousin's familiar voice: 'Hullo,' says Joachim, 'there you are!'

Roland Barthes speaks into the microphone on 7 January 1977. It is the day of the inaugural lecture, marking his appointment to Chair of Literary Semiology at the Collège de France. Towards the end of his address he'll speak of Thomas Mann's *The Magic Mountain*, and the strange age of his body. How he realized, upon rereading the novel the other day, that the tuberculosis he had experienced as a young man can't have been the current treatable version of the disease. How it was, down virtually to the last detail, the disease of the novel, which is set in 1907. Barthes will speak of rediscovering Mann's novel again the other day (for the purpose of preparing the lecture course on living-together he'd begin the following week), and realizing, quite suddenly, with a kind of stupefaction – the kind of stunned bewilderment, he says, that only the obvious can produce – that this made his body historical. In a sense, the contemporary of Hans Castorp's. Its age much older than his own age on that January day, which was sixty-one. What to do? This is the question that the lecture comes around to ask. What to do in this old and untimely body – now, in this new setting, on this new public stage, in what he'll call the new hospitality of the Collège de France? Forget, is the answer he'll offer. Forget and be carried forward by the force of forgetting, which is the forward-tilting force of all living life: forget the past, forget age, and press forward. Which is to say: begin again. Even, be born again. 'I must make myself younger than I am,' he'll say in Richard Howard's translation of the lecture. 'I must fling myself into the illusion that I am contemporary with the young bodies present before me.' And so, right here, before those young bodies and witnessed by them, start 'a new life' with new concerns, new urgencies, new desires. Already he'll have said: 'I sincerely believe that at the origin of teaching such

15

as this we must always locate a fantasy, which can vary from year to year.'

For a long time, the inaugural lecture was the only part of Barthes's Collège de France teachings available for reading: first published as *Leçon* in French in 1978, Richard Howard's translation was then included in Susan Sontag's *A Barthes Reader*, which appeared in 1982. The notes for the lecture course he'd begin a week later – that is, on 12 January 1977 – would not be published in French until 2003, and the English translation a further decade after that. These lags in publishing and translating that produce new readerships: bodies like my own, as yet unborn at the time of the lectures themselves, listening now to the sound files of the audio recordings, reading the notes, making them speak and be spoken to by – making them contemporary with – my own present moment. 'Who are my contemporaries?' Barthes would ask in a lecture delivered a few months later: 'Whom do I live with?' The calendar, telling only of the forward march of chronological time, is of little help. The way it brackets together work produced in the same set of years, as if shared historical context were the condition or the guarantor of a relationship. The way it holds more distantly dated relations apart. My copy of *The Magic Mountain* lies open next to Howard's translation of the inaugural lecture, the one that was delivered before a packed auditorium; all those young bodies, they must be older now, pressed together in their seats, the aisles, out into the corridors. 'I should probably begin with a consideration of the reasons which have led the Collège de France to receive a fellow of doubtful nature,' is how Barthes opened his address. Although that can't *really* have been what he said.

What then? What, *really*, did he say? Or, to put the question another way: What is it, exactly, that the translators are asking me to go along with? Not that Barthes's public discourse or that Mann's prose *should* appear in English – the idea that this is all wholly normal. I know, on some level, that it's not. I know that Mann wrote in German. I know – really, I know – that Barthes wrote and delivered this lecture in French, in Paris, at the Collège de France (he'll even speak, in the lecture, of what it is to speak in French). I know it in the sense that, if queried, I'd be likely to say: *Yes, yes, of course, I do realize this.* It's not quite that I am thinking, when I read Barthes's address in English, that this is all exactly as it should be. It's more that when it comes to writing and reading translations the question of what is wholly normal or truly plausible, of what was *really* said or written, gets suspended, slightly. The translator asks me to agree to its suspension. To suspend, or to suspend even further, my disbelief. This can't really have been what he said (Barthes spoke in French; he claimed to barely speak English at all); nevertheless, I'll go with it. In this sense, there's something from the outset speculative and, I would say, of the novelistic about the translator's project, whatever the genre of writing she is writing in. The translator asks us to go with the English of Joachim's greeting, the English of Barthes's lecture, in much – or is it exactly? – the same way as the fiction-writer asks us to credit the lake just visible from the station; to see rather than query the grey waters, how the firs on its shores are dense and then thin.

Here's a novel with a mountain on the cover. A novel set high up in the Swiss Alps, one of Germany's most formative contributions to modern European literature. I turn to the first chapter, the small opening paragraph: 'An unassuming young man was travelling, in midsummer, from his native city of Hamburg to Davos-Platz in the Canton of the Grisons, on a three weeks' visit.' And the magic of it is that I get caught up – to begin with unexpectedly, and then really quite quickly and for a long while caught up – with this journey, the steep and steady climb that never comes to an end. Which means that somewhere I must have already said: Yes. Okay, I accept. Look at me: I'm gone, I've gone with it.

'But there really is not room to dance,' she'll say – eventually, when I reach this scene. This strange, abruptly and extensively bilingual scene, marking the midway point of *The Magic Mountain*.

'Would you like to dance?' he'd asked, some pages after the exchange with the small silver pencil.

And then again: 'What do you say, shall we dance?'

'But there really is not room,' she'll reply. '*Et puis sur le tapis* –,' switching without warning from English to French and back again – 'Let us look on:'

In the scene I am reading, Clavdia Chauchat and Hans Castorp speak to one another in French. Which both presents and stages a problem:

'Winter is descending on Minnesota and I'm thinking I'd like to give Thomas Mann's *The Magic Mountain* a second reading,' writes a reader named nanojath. It's 8.19 p.m. on 29 October 2008 and he has just posted for advice on ask.com:

'Problem: in the translation I own, the extensive French dialog, most particularly in the Walpurgis-Night section (last section of Chapter 5) is not translated, and I don't speak French.

'I've looked for translations online a couple of times but this machine translation' – the link he provides is broken – 'is the best I've come up with, and although a reasonable amount of semantic content can be dredged out of that, it just won't do (for me) as a companion to reading the actual novel.

My ideal would be a proper literary translation I could grab online. Second choice would be input on translations that render this dialog in English, so I can troll around the local library system for a copy to photocopy the relevant section.

I really don't want to buy another copy of *The Magic Mountain.*'

This scene presents a problem – a translation problem whose solution here clearly presents a reading problem – but it also lays bare the fiction, the thin layer (or degree of slight separation?) of further fiction that the translation introduces and asks us to accept. (Fiction, writes Barthes – I'm paraphrasing here: like the transfers used in transfer-printing, like the technique of printing onto ceramics; 'a slight detachment, a slight separation which forms a complete, coloured picture, like a decalcomania.') To be clear, if Hans Castorp is prepared to address Clavdia Chauchat so hesitantly and uneasily in French, it is in the first place because he can: twenty years old, a serious young man in pre-War Europe, he could speak more than one European language, at least a little bit. But there's more to it than that. If Hans Castorp is prepared to announce, in French, his decision to address her in a language he doesn't speak well – *'moi, tu le remarques bien, je ne parle guère le français'* – speech-acting it, as the philosophers might call it: saying it and doing it at the same time. Here I am writing in English (so I am). Now I am writing in French (no, and this is the problem: no you're not). If he is actively choosing, in this moment of observing the dancing, the strange spectacle of the masked patients of the sanatorium, dancing now, on the carpet before them, it is because he prefers it: I prefer this language to my own, he says, *'je préfère cette langue à la mienne, car pour moi, parler français, c'est parler sans parler, en quelque manière – sans responsabilité, ou comme nous parlons dans un rêve. Tu comprends?'* It is because speaking in French, for him, is like speaking without speaking somehow. It is like speaking without responsibility – or in the way we speak in a dream. Do you see?

Yes, French. Addressing her, speaking with her, he prefers French – he *chooses* French.

22

But over what?

Over German. It would have to be German of course.

Of course, of course.

Suddenly, and as if for the first time, this scene makes me aware of the agreement I made. I come up against the belief I suspended:

So this was *never* in English, then. This was *always* in German.

And German as a language quite different from the French that the characters are now choosing to speak.

Or, this was always *supposed* to have been in German, and to be received as if it were still, somehow, in German, and *I did know this*, implicitly, even as I accepted the novel in English. This is the belief-suspension that reading a translation requires: even when all logics point to the characters speaking, acting and interacting, to the prose having been written, the feelings and ideas having been articulated, in German (the story of an unassuming young man making his way, in midsummer, from his native city of Hamburg to Davos-Platz), here it all is in English, and here I am being invited – expected? – to go with it.

And I do. Clearly, I do.

It's an everyday peculiar thing: an altogether obvious and necessary thing, only right now producing a whole new bewilderment.

And then it occurs to me: if the novel that Mann originally wrote in German has been translated, comprehensively, into English (since this is, after all, TRANSLATED FROM THE GERMAN, as the title page of my edition announces in full caps) then the long sections of French in this exchange can't have been translated at all. I mean, these passages, the lines of French that I have been copying out – which appear in French on the page, 'even in the English translation', as nanojath points out – can only be transcribed Thomas Mann.

The translator has lifted the French passages directly from the German edition and is hoping for enough familiarity on the part of her readers that they'll be capable of reading them.

Or, if not that, then enough goodwill on the part of her readers that they'll be willing to skim over them.

Then again, what else was she going to do?

A note. It's true. She might have translated the French into English and written a note, making us nod as we read: flagging up from the bottom of the page or somewhere else in the book that what we're about to read or have just read is/was said in French, the rest of it in German, and here is all of it in English. Which is what John E. Woods does in his retranslation of the novel, published in 1995. (The newer translation that jedicus, another ask. com poster, answering back from across the internet just twelve minutes later, will direct nanojath toward: have a look on Google Books, he suggests; there might be a few pages of the Woods translation missing, but you should now be able to read most of Chapter 5.)

Or italics. She might have translated the French into English and marked the difference between the English-translated-from-the-French and the English-translated-from-the-German in *italics*. Or a new font maybe, like in the dragon-training book I have been reading aloud to my sons at bedtime. When the hero speaks a bit of Dragonese, and in all the places where the dragons speak to one another in their peculiar deep-sea language, their words are written out in English but printed in something like 𝔄𝔡𝔬𝔟𝔢 𝔊𝔬𝔱𝔥𝔦𝔠. Which makes for an interesting evening conundrum: should I assume a dragon accent when I read the dragon bits aloud? Like the villains once did in the movies? Or should I just tell them, announcing as I read: right, okay, so, listen boys, you'll hear this bit in English, but since it's a dragon who's speaking, and speaking in a language that no human, bar the hero, is supposed to understand, what you'll truly be hearing, according to the logic of the book, is a kind of live instant translation. A bit like that scene in the Bible, the New Testament, which I realize that perhaps you don't know, but there's this scene where the Apostles speak and the miracle of it is that everyone hears their words as being spoken directly and simultaneously in their own languages, with no delay and with no interval. Speech multiplied and diversified but in this moment without difference – as a counter to the story of Babel, this time without it apparently making any difference. Or the scenes in Elena Ferrante's novels, the ones I have stacked in a pile by my bed, when her characters abruptly switch from Italian into dialect and back again but rather than producing passages of dialect on the page, Ferrante asks me to imagine it. Even in the Italian, so I learn from an interview with her translator Ann Goldstein, she asks her readers to imagine it. And to hear the switch, to hear the sudden change in cadence, in

26

vowel-sounds, in familiarity, in violence and in urgency, and in this instance to register what this switch means, and all the real and powerful difference it makes, but without actually seeing it or hearing it or reading it. And all these further invitations to suspend my disbelief, to note without having to contend with the very real and very material differences between these different languages, recalling somewhere, for me, a difficulty that Gilles Deleuze sets out at the beginning of an essay called (in Daniel W. Smith's translation) 'He Stuttered'. It has to do with dragons (really, it does. Or at least to my mind and on some level it does). It's often said that you can tell a bad novelist by his over-use of speech tags, writes Deleuze, in my memory of how the essay begins. You know, the kind of writer who wants to distinguish between his characters. But instead of introducing variety into their manners of speaking, will simply write: 'he murmured', 'he sobbed', 'he giggled' and so on. We can laugh at this, but in fact it's a tricky thing. Because, say you're a writer and you want your character to stutter. Or, say you're a writer and you want the dragons in your story to speak in some ancient icy reptile tongue. What do you do?

Well, it would appear that you can only do one of two things. Either, you can say it. You can say to your reader: this is how they speak. You can announce it. You can indicate the stutter, tagging it, but without actually performing it:

'No!' he stuttered. ('Yes!' iced the dragons, in their cold lizardy language, which no one bar the hero is supposed to understand.)

Or, you can write the stutter out. You can show the stuttering on the page, you can perform it, but without announcing it:

'N-n-n-n-o!' he said. ('Yes!' said the dragons.)

What else are you going to do?

In fact, it soon becomes clear that I don't need to do anything. My kids don't need me to keep reminding them of the dragon-difference. They've got it; they get it: this is what books do, Mum. Or, this is what good books do: they make us hear the different voices. They make us feel and in this way believe that they are written in different languages, in different orders of language here competing against each other, even when they appear to be, or when convention or convenience or the contested boundaries of so-called national literatures insist that they are written in just one. And they're right, of course they're right. And this might be somewhere along the way towards what Deleuze is saying in his essay too, in relation to what he'll come to offer as a third option available to or thrust by circumstance upon the writer, which would be neither to announce it, exactly, nor quite to perform it but to write in such a way that would make the language itself stutter. And stammer. To write – perhaps? – in the way Hans Castorp speaks French. How he can say, in English, 'Oh I speak German, even in French,' and I can see that this is true: that his hesitant and uneasy French does indeed appear to have been somehow modulated, patterned – stuttered? – by the difference of the other language, as well as his agitation, his nerves. I'd like to talk about all this a bit more: to find the passages in the dragon-training book where we think we can hear and feel the charge, the strange tremor of the 'dragon-speak' even when they're not actually speaking, where we feel that language itself has been made colder, or older. But you know, it's bedtime, and it's no surprise that my kids have not been listening for a while now. They were long ago already somewhere else: scaling the cliff-face above the sea, into the black cave with the bag for the hunt. I'm the one who wants them to pause on the threshold of believing for a moment, and think for a bit longer about how this translation pact works: the translator as necessarily invested in instating her own further fiction, and working to make it hold. Not because it is her all-purpose and always default intention to produce unremarkable English. To write German, or Italian or French prose again as if it had all been originally produced right here, and then to insist that this is all normal and how things should be. But for the prior reason that before we're in a position to register the strangeness, the stuttering or otherwise of the prose – the ways in which the project of translating Mann or Ferrante or Dragonese might put new pressures on the English language, forcing the discovery of new, or tapping into old and neglected resources. Which is to say: before we're even in a position to critique or worry over the decisions made by the translator, some provisional agreement has already been made. We have accepted the book in English. We have accepted that the book is now written in what appears to be English. The translator has made this thing that we now have at least minimally in common. And we share it – we are already sharing in it – in the most basic sense that we can at least now hold it and read it and copy out from it. I am a translator, responsible in part for the delayed appearance of Barthes's lecture notes in English: beginning work on translating the first Collège de France lecture course some thirty or so years after the fact. I am also an invested reader of books in translation, altogether willing to *go with* what the translator is asking me to accept. And it occurs to me that if I keep returning to this scene in *The Magic Mountain*, to this extraordinary scene of difference and desire as played out by the offsetting of one historical language against the other, and by speaking the one *inside* or *while at the same time* speaking the other, and with all of it happening for me in a third, it is because when reading translations I, too, seem to have trouble making myself pause, and registering for a moment. And registering not just like some box I might tick, unthinkingly, casually, on some webpage or other – yes okay *cookies*, yes okay *translation*, I get it, I've got it, I accept your terms – but to stop and *properly register*. With a small gasp in the course of reading. That if the French is still Mann's, lifted intact and unaltered from the German text in which it was once embedded. Then what this means. What this *also* means. What this *must also mean* is that all the pages of prose framing the conversation written in French. Which is to say, the whole novel: the great climb and descent of *The Magic Mountain*, including the midpoint sentences I read and wrote out above – I'm thinking again of the thin, dark silk. Yes, and – what was it? The soft fringes of her hair.

The slightly prominent bone at the back of her neck.

The amazingly white arms.

The mechanism with its hard little needle of lead – were handled by Helen Lowe-Porter.

We receive them twice-written; the second time by her.

~~DON'T~~ DO TRANSLATIONS

Don't do translations, I remember being advised, about a decade ago, by a well-meaning professor. At least, not if you're planning on making a living. Or, let's say, on getting a job in the university. It's a thankless thing, really. A 'little art,' Lowe-Porter called it, despite the great determining resonance her own work would have. You could try writing a monograph instead. Perhaps a monograph *about* translation. But don't spend your time, and certainly not all your time, on doing them.

The first time I heard the word *monograph* I wasn't exactly sure what it meant.

The dictionary offers 'a learned treatise on a small area of learning. Or a written account of a single thing'. Which makes things difficult. Because translating is not a small area of learning, and nor is a translation ever an uncomplicatedly single thing. But it turns out that academics use the word to mean something different, making the *mono*, the just one, refer not to the subject matter – which might be a vast area of learning, or a book about many things – but to how the book is written. A monograph is a book written by just one person: a singly-authored original contribution to knowledge.

Don't do translations, he said, a decade or so ago.

Not if you want. Well, what exactly?

What exactly did I want?

Now I think of it, a different question might have been: what is it that you have found in the practice of translation? That is, in the *writing* of literary translations – since, among all the many instances of translation currently happening everywhere and all the time in the world, this is the form your activity seems to take? What is it about this activity, in its difference from single-handed original authorship – the way it complicates the authorial position: sharing it, usurping it, sort of dislocating it. But the way it gets things said and written, heard and read nonetheless, by these other, more distributed means. *What is it* about the practice of writing translations? And how (in whose terms exactly?) do you propose to *properly register* what's going on with this – with your – work?

The American-born Helen Lowe-Porter began her translation career in the early 1920s. She was living in Oxford, married to a university professor and the mother of three daughters. As John C. Thirlwall describes it in his account of her relations with Thomas Mann (*In Another Language. A Record of the Thirty-Year Relationship between Thomas Mann and His English Translator, Helen Tracy Lowe-Porter*, published in 1966) 'she did not want to vegetate intellectually', and so had 'let it be known that she was available as a translator from Italian, French or German'. She was sent a copy of the German edition of Mann's *Buddenbrooks*; she read it and liked it. In her own article, 'On Translating Thomas Mann', published in 1950, she writes: 'to me personally *Buddenbrooks* was a welcome and delightful phenomenon'. Not at all sentimental; unlike so much of the work published in the wake of German Romanticism, here was 'emotion cooled off and served up on ice'. She began work on a translation and 'greatly enjoyed translating it'.

Early in 1924, Mann read parts of her work in progress and wrote in praise of her skill and sensitivity. He suggested that they meet. Perhaps he and Frau Mann could drop in to see her in Oxford? But they didn't specify a date. As a result, when they did turn up, no one was at home; the Manns had to wait. Lowe-Porter imagines them passing the time: 'I feel sure T. Mann looked over all the books in our scanty library ... and did his best to size up this unknown instrument which – due to the vicissitudes of those war and postwar years – must willy-nilly (and of course unless he could find a better one) serve him to change the garment of his art into a better one which might clothe her for the market place until times changed.' The translator as an unknown instrument: a tool to be used, a service provider, engaged in undressing and carefully re-dressing the literary work of art for the purposes of a new market. Like a lady's maid. I know nothing, really, about lady's maids, other than what I've seen in period dramas on the TV, but this is the first image that springs to mind. Like a lady's maid who corresponded with Albert Einstein, Herman Broch and Theodor Adorno. An unknown instrument who was 'known throughout her life for her passionate interest in literature and her outspoken liberal views', as David Horton describes her in his recent book *Thomas Mann in English*. A stay-at-home mother of three who deliberately sought out complex translation work as a means to challenge herself intellectually. Only apparently to downplay its complexity, its intellectual challenge, in a published account of her work (let me just change the garment of your art...).

Then aged forty-four, Helen Lowe-Porter would continue work on the translations of Mann's books for the next twenty or so years, stopping only in her late sixties, partly because of ill health and partly to pursue, and to resume, her own literary projects: poems, a play. Her translations would be extraordinarily successful in the new marketplace: fast-selling, popular with the reading public and the means by which Thomas Mann would secure his reputation as 'one of the leading German novelists of the twentieth century', which is how Todd Kontje puts it in the preface to the *Cambridge Introduction to Thomas Mann*, as well as 'one of the few to transcend national and language boundaries to achieve major stature in the English-speaking world'. A line quoted by David Horton, who makes the point that this 'major stature is to a very large extent the direct result of the efforts of his authorized translator'. New versions of Mann's works have appeared in the years since Knopf's claim on the rights expired in the 1970s, but Lowe-Porter's work is still everywhere in print.

I read *The Magic Mountain* in Lowe-Porter's translation, as part of the project of translating Barthes's *Comment vivre ensemble*, the lecture course he began a week after the inaugural lecture, which in English is titled *How to Live Together*. My copy of the novel is a bit battered now – the cover is creased. One long crease runs up the front of it like a life-line, past the bright cluster of buildings foregrounded at the base of a mountain, through the black fir forest above them, scaling the greyer, more distant peak beyond it and then up and out into the white sky and off the uppermost edge of the book. *The Magic Mountain*, with its structured sanatorium-living, is a key text for Barthes in the lecture course, one of a small selection of tutor texts – or *textes d'appui* as he calls them. Supporting texts: the texts that brace us, the ones we lean on, testing them to see if they'll support our weight; the texts we always seem to be in conversation with, whether directly or indirectly; the texts that enable us to say or write anything at all. Every discourse, says Barthes, is generated and sustained by its own more or less idiosyncratic, imperfectly remembered selection. This is not so much a comment as a principle. 'There is an age at which we teach what we know,' he'd said in the inaugural lecture. 'Then comes another age at which we teach what we do not know; this is called research.' In this digressive, excursive teaching ('research, not a lecture,' he'll stress at the end of the first session), the practice was never to be exhaustive, or systematic: to work or walk in a straight line toward some generalizing theory, an ultimate grand idea. Instead, to set down a fantasy. And then to induce from the fantasy, a research project. The fantasy for this year of a form of living together that would accommodate rather than dictate the individual rhythms of its small-scale community. Allowing for something like solitude, as Barthes puts it, with regular interruptions. What kinds of structures, spatial or temporal, would enable this? Where to look for suggestion and detail, for models and counter-models that could be simulated, or already find their part-equivalents, in life? As materials to think with, Barthes compiles this unlikely corpus – an unexpected collection of writings and novels: *The Magic Mountain*, *Robinson Crusoe*, the texts of the Desert Fathers, Zola's novel set in an apartment building, André Gide's account of the real-life sequestered woman of Poitiers. The inquiry will proceed sketchily, says Barthes. Each lecture will offer just a few lines of approach; open a few possible dossiers. I'll only be marking out the contours of these zones of interest. Like the squares on a chequerboard, he says, which perhaps one day I'll fill in. Marking out the spaces, setting the places. A place for animals. Also for bureaucracy, for flowers and for food. I see it like a table: seating you next to you and you next to you, anticipating the conversations between topics, the arguments. The invitation to his audience was to collaborate actively in the inquiry. To fill in the suggested squares themselves, or to propose new ones. And they did: they spoke with Barthes between the sessions, or left notes, and wrote letters, asking questions, making corrections, providing alternative references, redirecting the path of the research toward their own different concerns, which might be one way of describing to myself what I think I am doing here.

It is easy not to think about translation. This has to do, of course, with the way translations typically get presented to readers: the name of the original author in full caps and bold; the translator's name smaller or left off the cover altogether; reviewers failing to register the fact of reading in and the creative labour of translation. But perhaps it also has to do with the way we tend to talk about – and so also experience? – prose translations. That is, prose translations, as provisionally distinct from all the other ways an existing work of art can be reproduced, remediated or re-versioned. From all the many other practices of redoing, rewriting and remaking – of working with extant material – with which the writing of translations in the so-called 'standard' sense is always proximate and talking to, sharing gestures and problematics, but with which it is not, I don't think, wholly interchangeable. The point is this: unlike those other re-mediations, which might require us to acknowledge the difference of their new materials as well as the intervention, the new gesture, of their reproducer, translations seem to give us the permission to say, quite unworriedly: that book? Yeah, I've read it. They give us the permission, or we take it. I've read Mann's novels. I've read *Buddenbrooks* and *The Magic Mountain*, but not *Doctor Faustus*, or the *Joseph* books. I've read most of Flaubert. I've read Ferrante. And I really like her work a lot. I've read Barthes. It's true that I might sometimes qualify this. I might say (or hear other people say): actually, no. You haven't. You haven't *really* read Barthes, for example, until you've read his work in French. But more often than not the possibility of reading in French is offered as a kind of surplus value. As in: there is reading. Yes, agreed. Let's hold to that: there is something like the baseline of reading that is made possible by translation. And then, added to that, there is the *additional* value of reading *in the original*. Does the first assertion, the first reading experience, always have the other somewhere in mind? This is the question that Gérard Genette asks, briefly, in a book called *The Work of Art*, translated by G. M. Goshgarian. Or, to put the question another way: imagine I were to tell you that *The Magic Mountain* is in the living room. Imagine. The reason why you're not a bit bewildered by this is because we both know – we both seem to already know – that what I *really* mean to say (what the work of metonymy is enabling me to say) is *the novel* is in the living room: my copy, our copy or someone else's copy of the novel is in the living room. Does something of the same order happen when talking about the books I've read? When I tell you that I have read *The Magic Mountain* is this a quick small-part-for-the-whole way for me to tell you that I've read *The Magic Mountain* in English translation? The title here standing in for the translation which, in its own complicated way, is standing in for the original – each slightly smaller, reduced part (the title, the translation) pointing to some further, just out of reach and more expansive aesthetic experience (the real one this time, the authentic one)? Talking with you about the books I've read, and affirming that I have read them, is this what I mean?

Possibly. Or, no. That is, I don't think so.

Unlike me, you may have read Mann's novel in the German, and I'm very interested to know what that's like. I'm also very inclined to agree that there's great value in reading in the original. Perhaps something like the value we recognize and invest in literature. The right words in the right order, as Virginia Woolf puts it so simply in her talk on craftsmanship, delivered over the radio in 1937. These necessary words, in this necessary order. There is literature, arguably, or what we call the literary, when this matters: when we feel like something would be wrong should ever these words or their ordering be changed (if Clarissa Dalloway were to buy gloves and not the flowers herself, for example, as she does in an early draft of the novel). In this sense, literary translation, as a labour of changing words, and changing the orders of words, is always and from the outset wrong: its wrongness is a way of indirectly stressing and restressing the rightness of the original words in their right and original order. Translation operates, then, as a kind of vital test: an ever-renewable demonstration of the literary value of the novel in German. Which is one way of saying that literature, that quality we call the literary, simply cannot do without translation as a means of repeatedly reaffirming it (and when the words of a translation matter in turn, when we feel, in a translation, that it must indeed be these necessary words in this necessary order, the translation has become literature too). The theorist and critic Derek Attridge has written at length about the complex ways our sense of the identity of a work of literature requires, on the one hand, repetition (the repetition of what he calls 'these specific words in this specific arrangement' across all material supports: whether the book is read online or on paper or out loud, whether it is printed in this font or that, we are still able to identify it as the same work) and, on the other, an openness to just how non-identical the different manifestations of (and the forms of my engagement with) apparently the same work can be. How, in fact, the font does matter, or it can – likewise the timing and circumstances of my reading, the books I am reading the book with, the people I am talking to about it, who might make me think differently; the difference between reading a book for the first time and for the third. 'Literary identity,' he writes, 'involves both repetition of what is recognized as "the same" and openness to new contexts and hence to change'. In other words, to translation. Which might go some way towards explaining why, even with my keen interest in the original, I still believe – I still feel reluctant to qualify my basic conviction – that when it comes to this novel I, too, have read it. A belief that would appear to get stronger, and even more solid in its foundation, the further away from the original language I feel. Perhaps you'll hear me say that there are works in French I haven't truly? or fully? or properly? read because I have only? read them in translation, but that's surely premised on the chance, the plausibility, of one day reading the originals. Mann on the other hand? Tolstoy? Ferrante? Kang? All those books? Yes, I've read them. Or, let me maintain that I have read them. Let me believe that what I have read in English partakes, in all its difference, of what you have read in German, in Russian, in Italian, in Korean. This, after all, has been the form of my aesthetic experience, my own expansive and authentic aesthetic experience. I notice that the more remote the languages seem from my own capacity to learn them, the more assertive I feel. Why is this? I am more willing to register and be troubled by the closer, familiar differences than the more distant ones, I realize, and perhaps this is complicatedly true of all of us: when we are presented with a version of something that we know we can't know, or not without some great, unlikely effort on our part, we are more prepared to accept how it comes, and to grow attached to the only form in which we are able to receive it. An English-speaking friend tells me about reading Calvino, a writer whom he loves, *Cosmicomics* in particular, and how often he goes back to read the stories that make up that book, and how badly he wants to believe – and, in fact, the degree to which he does believe, despite the translator's name on the frontispiece – that it was Italo Calvino who handled the words that he is now reading, who wrote them *for him*. A naïve misconception (or an active self-deception?) on many levels, you might say: this Romantic attachment to monographic, single-handed authorship, this fantasy of unmediated address, and with it – underlying it and enabling it – my friend's serene failure to notice, let alone to name the translator. One that he could easily think his way out of, if he wanted to (I look it up for him: *Cosmicomics* was translated by William Weaver in 1968). But worth taking seriously. A common reading experience enabled by translation that I think it's very important to take seriously. If only because, well, there he is, my reading friend: sitting on his own in a chair with a book. Reading, alone and for the moment uninterruptedly, for some hours at a time. There he is, and this is what he's thinking, and this is how he feels.

The translator: writer of new sentences on the close basis of others, producer of relations. In the first instance, of her own personal relation with the books she reads and undertakes to translate. As well as with the writer she often thinks of – even, with whom she corresponds, if correspondence is possible – as she works. Then, the complex relations between the writing she has written and the extant writing that was the condition of her producing it. The translation theorist and scholar Theo Hermans has recently argued for the performative power of the speech act that declares *this is a translation*, thus bringing with it – or right here and now making – a complicated 'promise of representation'. A translation becomes a translation only when someone (the translator, the publisher, the reader, an institution) declares it to be one; up until that point, writes Hermans, the status of her writing is 'merely another text'. I like this argument a lot. Not because I think the person writing a translation is likely to think of what she is writing as 'merely another text'. (Certainly, in my own case, I am always and from the outset privately declaring – if only to an audience of myself – the sentences I am writing to be translations: it is this understanding and framing of what I am doing that shapes the kinds of sentences I am able to write.) But because Hermans's argument leaves the door wide open for the later – the later, or at least differently timed – declaration that says, retroactively or projectively: *this* is actually a translation of *that*. And in this way works as invitation to think further about how, in the wake of such a declaration – should indeed the declaration be heard, should indeed it be registered at all (think of my reading friend, communing directly with Calvino) – so many things change: our manners of reading change, our whole orientation towards what we're reading changes, as in a brilliantly simple and provocative exercise I once observed a student set our translation class. She gave the group an original piece of writing and its translation, but had privately made them swap places. So what we read was an excerpt from a novel originally published in English but presented to us as if it were a translation from the French. Everyone was predictably critical of the English (in other words the original), finding it to be in different ways poorly written, misjudged, mistaken with regards to the rightness of the French (which was actually the translation). Everyone was a bit flushed and affronted, quickly backtracking when the trick of the exercise was revealed. Which suggests that rather than testifying to any identifiable quality of the prose itself, the categories of 'original' and 'translation' act more like placeholders: 'original' and 'translation' are the names for the positions we put writing in, and for the histories of writing labour we then assign to them (first-time writing, second-time writing). Positions which can then orientate and determine, in quite striking ways, the way the writing gets read. As in the sequence which closes Anne Carson's *Nay Rather,* an essay on translation, where the familiar stops and signs from the London Underground, collected and sequenced, are thereby pronounced a translation of the Greek poet Ibykos's fragment 286; and, on the facing page, the lines taken and set out from pages 136-7 of *Conversations with Kafka* by Gustav Janouch are likewise thereby pronounced a translation of that same fragment; and, turning the page again, so too are the words lifted from pages 17-18 of *The Owner's Manual* of her new Emerson 1000w microwave oven. Carson calls this – the project of 'translating a small fragment of ancient Greek lyric poetry over and over again using the wrong words' – not exactly an exercise in translating, nor even an exercise in untranslating, but more like a 'catastrophizing of translation'. She also calls it 'a sort of stammering'.

This is a translation!

Is it? I feel sure that something would happen – some adjustment to your reading manner would be very likely to occur – if you were to hear me all of a sudden insisting that it is.

Declaring her work to be a translation, and in this way inviting the world to read her writing as a translation, the translator instates a particular – certainly temporal, and for this reason very often hierarchical – relation between two writings (one then two, first then second, *that* absent work which gave direct and close rise to *this*), one of which she may think of as hers. In this way, she gets involved with you. The translator collaborates with the prose she is translating, with the publisher, and let's say, also, with *time*, with the moment of her work and the new circumstances in which it appears, to enable your relation to the book, your sense of what it is, and of how it was written, and the person or people who wrote it. As a part of this, you might form a relation with her, with me. In the way that the more I think about the midway scene in *The Magic Mountain* (the more I wonder about the problematics of translating this scene), my relation feels increasingly to be with Lowe-Porter. Typically, though, the relation you'll form is with the writer – your sense of the writer – who wrote the book first. If my friend feels the way he does about Calvino (about Calvino and not Weaver), it is because translation makes this possible: it is precisely this chance of forming a reading relation with a writer writing in another language that a translation, making no official claim to original authorship, *also* produces. You might form a relation with her, with me, as you read and depend on or query my translations. Though typically it is more likely to be with him. But what is most difficult, it seems, is both. Not either/or, but holding and maintaining a relation with both writers, a sense of both writing practices, in their shared project and in all the important ways those projects differ, in the head, and somehow together.

There's a moment in Barthes's last lecture course – the last two-part course he would give at the Collège de France, beginning in 1978. The course on the novel, in which Barthes makes a two-year series of public lectures out of a private writing project, turning the space of the lecture into a kind of performed working-out of his sudden late-in-life desire for a new life, which for him, he says, could only take the form of a new writing practice: this fantasy of writing a novel, prompted directly by the recent and devastating death of his mother. The last course he gave, but the first one I read, in lecture note-form, when the notes were published in French in 2003. The one I pitched to translate, feeling so caught up in my own relation to the course, to Barthes's slow setting out of the circumstances under which a novel might get written (by him, in the late 1970s, but also, in principle, by any one of those young bodies listening at the time, any one of us who might today, in our own present bodies, share something of that desire), and thinking of – fantasizing – the process of translating the course as one way – one drawn-out, especially attentive way – of *taking it* such a long time after the fact. There's a section of the course that was drafted, but when it came to it never delivered. Perhaps because Barthes's microphone had not been working the week before? And so when it came to lecturing from his notes on this section he needed to go a bit faster. In this skipped bit of the course, Barthes had prepared to talk about his renewed interest in the author, in the life lived by the author, in his or her biographical circumstances. In other words: in what kind of person, in what kind of body and in what kind of context the author was writing and how they might have been thinking about what they were trying to do. Which is funny, and perhaps surprising, given how famous his 'Death of the Author' essay still is. There was this whole period in the 1960s, notes Barthes, marked by a kind of incuriosity with regard to the life, the circumstances of the author, and the article I wrote was a part of that. But now? Now I feel a bit differently. Now things have changed. In fact, he writes, I feel this curiosity developing freely in me. No doubt this comes as part of the project of writing a novel, conceived here in the form of a lecture course, where the question is also, and for Barthes really has to be: what kind of life would enable a person to write such a long stretch of continuous prose? And indeed how to live it? What settings, what relations, what personal circumstances? Even: what writing tools (what pens, what paper?), what kind of desk orientation and organization would enable the living of it? Barthes describes a newfound preference for reading about the lives of certain writers over the works they produced (I know Janouch's *Conversations with Kafka* better than Kafka's work, he notes; Tolstoy's *Carnets* better than the rest of Tolstoy). How inconsistent: this about-turn. This late change of position. Yes, notes Barthes, indirectly, a bit later on in the same session. Yes and true. But this precisely is the point: I'm not immobile (which might be one way of restating the point of the 'Death of the Author' essay, too). Neither I nor the writing I have published is immobile. And yet it's something people seem to find very hard to accept. I've noticed how some people, PhD students especially, will fall out of contact for a few years – which is of course to be expected. Only to all of a sudden call you up: out of nowhere, they want you to be on their jury, engage with their work. They have no real interest in you, of course: in who you might have become. They want you to still be exactly as you were, in the same place, in the position where they left you: talking about the death of the author, about myth, about the language of fashion. But I no longer have anything whatsoever to say about fashion! There's an aggressiveness to this attitude, in this assumption that I haven't – that surely I can't have – moved. They'll lose touch for five years and then expect to find me again, whenever they feel like calling me up, in the same chair, waiting by the phone. Which is to say: we all think of the other as available, as always on hand. I do it too, probably. Of course. But in reality, my drive, my fantasy is to change places, to be reborn. Which means: I'm never where you want me to be.

I –

Which I now? Barthes, or me?

me: the translator, testing out and writing into a new translation of the recording of this lecture all these decades later, heartbeat racing in an effort to get this right: Barthes waiting by the telephone. Or not. No, and this is the thing: he's somewhere else, interested and investing in something else. I think of Renee Gladman, poet, novelist and translator, asking her interviewer in an interview: 'When you're reading translations, don't you sometimes feel the racing heartbeat of the translator trying to get shit right?' Trying, in my case, to arrive at a new phrasing for Barthes's beautifully unlaboured sentence: *on pense toujours aux autres à disposition*. For what Jonathan Culler calls his 'preference for loose and evasive appositional syntax', especially in the later work. Whereby, as Elizabeth W. Bruss explains, the emphasis would so often be made to 'fall more heavily on the individual word'. And 'especially on its shimmering capacity to mean many different and inconsistent things at once, once syntax no longer constrains it to a single value'. Trying to find – Why not? (I know why, but just for the moment): Why not? – something like a new dress for it, a new thing for it to wear, to appear publicly in: we always think of others as available, on hand, to hand, at our service and disposal. Trying to get it right. While at the same time having to elaborate my own provisional and for the moment personal understanding of what *right* means in this case, in the particular scenario of this sentence, which might very well be different from the one that came before. And the question is: Well, do you? Do I? Reading translations, is this the kind of heat that you – or indeed I – want to feel? Or no, not really, not at all? It's easy not to think about translation and translators. It's easy not to bear the translator in mind, to hold the thought of her, the history of her work, in the head, while reading. She might have a great deal of investment in enabling your close relation with some idea of the writer whose sentences she too has written, only this time in a language you can read; she might have a great deal of investment in you investing in the ventured rightness of her new phrasing, and this in itself – the pull of the sentences she has written, and what they call forth – can serve to distract you from her. But then again, without this sometime effort (perhaps no more effortful than thinking of two things at once, or flickering intermittently between the two?), how else to make the interest of her practice, its racing heartbeat, the very case for doing it, appear?

Don't do translations. It's not really such a great idea to, the professor said. Although I like to think that the advice would be different now. Now that Translation Studies is an established field, and the practice of translation is taught as part of its many university programmes; now that academics have the possibility, at least in theory, of submitting translations as evidence of their research. And there are independent presses dedicated to publishing translations, and literary journals, in print and online, likewise committed to the dissemination of work in translation. Now that we can read articles in the book pages of the paper pointing to the extraordinary recent success of Karl Ove Knausgaard's novels, translated into English by Don Bartlett, and of Elena Ferrante's body of work in Goldstein's translations. Now that we can apply for translator's grants and residencies, even share writers' prizes. There is still the pressing question of how to make a living as a literary translator, and the fact that translations still make up only the smallest percentages of the books that get published in English each year (what Chad W. Post has termed 'the three per cent problem'). But still. Let's agree that, relatively speaking: 'it's boom-time for translated fiction,' as Rachel Cooke announced in the *Observer*.

It's also, I don't know, *boom*-time. Cooke's article celebrating the 'subtle art of translating foreign fiction' was published on 24 July 2016. Exactly a month and a day after the UK vote to leave the European Union; what sounded, to my ear, as to so many others, like a great big boom.

It was a huge deal, on the scale of my life, to move, at nineteen, to a city in another country. Not very far away, only to France, a place I'd been going on holiday since I was a child. But even so: this time to the south of it. It was massive, formatively speaking, to take a train with my dad up to London, then to Paris, a metro across the city with all my things, and then down the length of the country from Montparnasse. For Dad to figure out the door-code, buy me a new duvet, some food for the fridge, all those simple loving things, and then say goodbye in the flat on the Rue Gambetta, setting me off on my Erasmus year abroad, before doing the same journey again in reverse. For me to venture out onto the place du Capitole. Find a seat in the pink brickwork, and feel the heat still in the walls. In October! In late November, even! I'd still be sitting out, my head thick with the peculiar kind of head-buzz that you only get from operating all day for the first time in another language, marvelling at how already it seemed to be creeping into my dreams. There was lots of that: trying to talk in new ways to new people. But never – not once – did it occur to me, nor, I don't think, to any of us in Toulouse, in Montpellier or Paris, in Rome, Munich or Madrid that what we were doing was *especially* special; or, let's say, provisional. We took it – our British middle-class mobility, the passage-rite of a year abroad, the very basically motivating idea that there might be some point, some personal and common interest, in learning and living and moving for a while in another language – for granted. There was no thought, then, for us in our privilege, that these conditions might turn out to be revocable: from normal to some erstwhile normality that I don't want to be – that I refuse to already be – reminiscing about.

Do translations! This is the invitation I want to make, relaying and rephrasing – deliberately countering – the advice I once received. Yes, yes and absolutely. Do translations, for the simple reason that we need them. We need translations, urgently: it is through translation that we are able to reach the literatures written in the languages we don't or can't read, from the places where we don't or can't live, offering us the chance of understanding as well as the necessary and instructive experience of failing to understand them, of being confused and challenged by them. We receive these books newly made by the hands of translators, and the small contacts that those hands make, between translator and writer, reader and translator, language and language, culture and culture, experience and experience are, as Edith Grossman puts it, as vital to our continued reading and writing, to the vitality of our languages, our cultures and experiences as the books themselves.

I look about me for all the small contacts translation makes: putting one book literally in touch with another, their faces smashed against each other in the pile by my bed. Or on my desk. Or, with less pressure: the one leaning into the other, supporting the other, on my shelves.

Contacts that fray pathways: there is a character in *The Magic Mountain*, a Mexican woman called *Tous-les-deux*. She is called *Tous-les-deux* in the German, too. One of her sons is dying of tuberculosis and now the other, who'd come to the sanatorium only for a short stay, has fallen ill as well. Both of them. Can you believe it? Both of them. She wanders the corridors of the novel, wondering at it, despairing at it, muttering it to herself: *tous les deux...* What sad sadness. Hence her name. A nickname, a pet name that the patients of the sanatorium make up for her, a borrowed new name that passes untouched from the German, where it first appears in 1924, into the French translation in 1931; a name that, following a different route, makes its way intact into the English translation in 1927. A pet name that is picked up, turned over, and held up to the light by Roland Barthes at the close of a lecture on names in 1977. Barthes read the novel in Maurice Betz's translation, and I'm told that in French the midway scene is this most extraordinary thing: the abrupt decision to switch into speaking French in the context of what is already a French translation, the uneasy, hesitant and a little bit mistaken French that Mann had written for Hans Castorp appearing italicized and intact ('reproduced without modifications', writes Betz in his translator's note) amidst all the other French. And 'the fascinating thing is,' writes Antoine Berman, in a piece translated by Lawrence Venuti, 'the young German's French is *not the same* as the young Russian woman's. In the translation, the two varieties of French are in turn framed by the translator's French. Maurice Betz let Thomas Mann's German resonate in his translation to such an extent that three kinds of French can be distinguished, and each possesses its specific foreignness.' *Tous-les-deux*: in spring 2013 the name reappears as the subject heading of an email exchange between this translator and the copy-editor of her translations: should we leave it French? In this English translation of Barthes's lecture notes, should we leave the name in French as Lowe-Porter did, and as Betz necessarily did? As a way of briefly telescoping the distances and making visible the paths between his work, her work, his work and our own?

We need translations. The world, the English-speaking world, needs translations. Clearly and urgently it does; we do. And this has to be a compelling argument for doing them.

But, I wonder: is it really *for the world* that the translator translates?

Primarily, I mean? Straightforwardly?

The translator takes the world by the back of the head. She leans in, pulling the English-speaking world in with her. She goes brow to brow with the world. And with breath hot and earnest against its face she says: *Look, world, I am doing this for you.*

Is that how it goes?

Well and why not?

Writing a translation can be a means to interrupt, to stall and expose the small-mindedness of the move I just made: the English-speaking world is not the world. It doesn't stand in for and is not equal to the world; its literature is not literature, its philosophy is not philosophy. The translations we do read are their own necessary reminder of this – of everything we are not reading, and yet has been written and is being read by so many others, vast populations of other writers and readers, all the time and everywhere else. I don't mean to suggest that translating for others, for the sake of the author or for future readers can't be motivation enough. But rather to ask, at a time when translation is still so broadly considered to be the most 'selfless' art, the most uncomplicatedly generous and self-sacrificing of all the arts, involving, apparently, the *least* of the practitioner's own self (except, perhaps, when it's thought to have been done badly) and therefore, also, so the thinking seems to go, the *least* 'art': What is it that makes this activity interesting *for the translator*? What are the features of this practice of translating that invite and challenge and sustain her? Before the translation reaches the world – and for the short time, or the long time, the days or years of time, it can take to write one?

There's a book on the table by the window. Let's say it's my table, by my window, the one I work on at home. Outside, there are trees, a café at the crossroads, the blue neon of King Kebab. There's the sound of traffic, buses and road-sweepers; schoolchildren walking in a crocodile on their way back from the swimming pool. Sometimes, on warm days, there are teenagers: small groups of mostly young men, late teens, early twenties. They gather on the concrete walls on either side of the steps leading up to the raised shopping area that my thirty-one-storey block sort of floats on – that it was designed to float on. A brutalist housing experiment completed in 1974, the cars pass around and underneath us on a lower-level road, turning the raised precinct, with its towers, its concrete planters, its school and its shops into an island for pedestrians. I am on the second floor, and from my table I can see them clearly: they pace along the lengths of the tops of the walls, or stand balanced on the edge. They wear headphones: music for focus and concentration. They pace the lengths of the tops of the walls to either side of the gap, or stand balanced on the edge, eyeing the one opposite. They pause, ready up, lean into their toes. But no. Not now, not quite. And then every so often they'll leap. Leap clean across the steps falling beneath them and land softly – always soft and easy like the clothes they wear – on the concrete shelf on the other side. If you happened to be walking up the steps at that moment, you might look up to see a boy fly – literally, for a moment, fly – over your head. *Parkour* practice, the ordinary outdoor breathtaking spectacle of it; meanwhile, on the table, there is this book. Or, not exactly a book. Not accurately a book – in the sense that Barthes's lectures were never intended to be published as books. In the last lecture course he speaks briefly about publishing the notes from the previous year.

How he had considered it, but in the end decided not to. Why? Partly, he says, because to do so would have been to manage and market the past. To repeat what had already been said ('I wrote *Mythologies* twenty years ago and I'm always asked for more mythologies. I wrote *The Pleasure of the Text* and what I still get asked is to say something about the pleasure of the text'). When the desire was very urgently to go forward, to press ahead, into a new activity, 'to work while there is still light'. But partly also because in a life's work 'there must always be a share for the ephemeral: for what happened once and fades'. A lecture, he says, is a specific kind of production: 'to my mind, neither wholly writing nor wholly speech but marked by an implicit interlocution (a silent complicity)'. A public lecture, openly offered, ventured speech, writing written for the lifespan of saying it out loud, is something that must and wants to die. Like a flower, he says. *Le cours c'est comme une fleur, vous permettez, mais qui va passer.* This is the sentence that Barthes wrote down in preparation for the lecture – I can read it now, published and eternal in French, in the book of lecture notes resting on my table. I would like to offer a translation of it. I am poised on the point of attempting a new translation of it.

And I realize that there's no obvious or necessary connection between my own activity and the boys outside.

It's simply, haphazardly, one of circumstance.

I want, however, to make something out of it: to link their stillness, their concentration, to the way the task of translation effects a similar slowing down. The translator, with her face in a funnel, her focus trained on this one book, and for the moment just this one sentence of the book, to the short-term exclusion of all the others. How, for this reason, the writing of a translation has its own particular duration which can't be accelerated – and that is different from the tempos of productivity we find elsewhere. I think this is important. Translation demands a certain, un-condensable, time *with a work* and therefore, also, with the questions animating that work, the questions the translator brings to it and the further questions that will inevitably arise from the gestures of translating it.

I sense and would like to venture some connection between the outdoor leaping (and fathoming out how to land) and my own anxiety over where and how to set down this *vous permettez* in English. (*Le cours c'est comme une fleur, vous permettez, mais qui va passer*). Because this, too, seems to me to be important: contributing to the particular tone and manner of Barthes's address, its warmth, its invitation to complicity, its quality of what he'll call 'non-arrogance': a form of discourse that puts no pressure on anyone else. And yet none of the options I can think of at the moment – *if you will*, or *if you'll allow me*, or *if I may* or *indulge me on this* or *as it were* or *so to speak*, with their varying degrees of self-conscious and knowing self-awareness – feel quite open or inviting enough, quite unaffected or *non-arrogant* enough.

Or, indeed, later on – what already feels like much later on in this short sentence – the matter of the final verb. People can pass in English, I know, as a manner of dying. But can flowers? They wilt, they fade; they can droop, wither and die. But can they pass? I don't know. I don't think so.

And it is here, with this not-knowing – not, for the moment, having any real idea of what to do, of how to proceed – that the temporary connection I'm trying to make disengages entirely. Because the fact is, I've watched the parkour boys a lot, catching sight of them bobbing on their ledge, getting shouted at and dispersed like pigeons, sometimes, by a shouty passerby. And it strikes me that they know exactly what they're doing: they've measured (pacing them out), the gaps they plan to jump. They've practised on the ground, with no steps falling beneath them; they've done this any number of times, as a way of ensuring that when it comes to it they'll make it. This sentence, on the other hand: I am able to read it, I feel fairly sure that I understand it. But until I start translating it, I'm not yet in a position to tell you exactly where, of what order or of what combination of orders (lexical, syntactical, atmospheric, psychological, ethical...), its difficulties will turn out to be. In this sense, I'm not sure I could practise for them. This not knowing – this not knowing ahead of time, ahead of engaging with the actual doing of it – is a source of – what? Excitement, I'd call it. Great nervous excited excitement. I feel this is important too. Because it is this process of discovery, this adventuring into the writing of a sentence, with no clear idea of what will happen when I start to try, that makes for the real, lived-out difference between reading a sentence – even reading a sentence and speculating in advance how I *might* go about translating it – and the concrete task of writing it in my own language, again.

The course is like a flower

There is the tight focus of the translator's attention, her face deep in the open-end of a funnel, trained at such narrow length on this one book, and for the moment on just this one line of the book, to the exclusion of all the others.

A lecture course, it is like a

The lecture course, it's like a flower,

There is the sentence that she is focused on, and the way the action of translating it, of touching it in this way, makes it start to unfold, to open out into a series of discrete or connected questions and challenges, in ways I don't believe it's possible for anyone to altogether foresee.

The course, if I may, is like a flower, but that will fade away.

A lecture course is   will die away.

And then there's the fact that the sentence won't refold – it won't re-compact, won't return to anything like its original tight or very lightly gathered economy – until she has found a way to answer each of them. Answers slowly elaborated over here, in the form of a new sentence.

Then, a great sequence of sentences.

That said, if I can propose directing the focus into the room in this way, onto the table and the activity it supports. If I can think of relating the world to the translator's work, rather than intend her work for the world. If I can think of holding the world and whatever it might want or need at bay for a while, ignoring it, at least for the time it takes to write my translations, to engage in the more private practice of it, with all the dailyness and exercise and ongoingness that the word implies, it is likely to be because my window gives on to one of the world's richest cities. It is surely because I translate from French into English, two world-dominant languages. It is because I am translating a much-read European theorist, critic, writer whose value is already assured, from a cultural tradition whose value is already assured, whose work had already been translated by very respected others, and for whom there were and still are readers waiting. 'Who we choose to translate is political,' write Antena in their 'Manifesto for Ultratranslation'. 'How we choose to translate is political.' Translation, then, as a form of activism: we need to vary our choices, argues John Keene in an essay titled 'Translating Poetry, Translating Blackness', we need 'more translation of literary works by non-Anglophone black diasporic authors into English' to be published in America. He writes: 'I believe too that we should have far more translations in general of work from outside the European and European-language sphere, more translations of work by women, by LGBTQ peoples, by Indigenous writers, by working class and poor writers, by writers with disabilities, and so on.' Doing such varied work is its own powerful way of doing politics.

It might also be because I have misunderstood where the world is. 'Imagine,' says Barthes, in the inaugural lecture, 'if by some unimaginable excess of socialism or barbarism, all but one of our disciplines were to be expelled by our educational system, it is the discipline of literature which would have to be saved, for all knowledge, all the sciences are present in the literary monument'. Think, he says, of a novel like Defoe's *Robinson Crusoe*, and of what it knows, all the fields of knowledge it accommodates in its pages: historical, geographical, social (violent and colonial), technological, botanical, anthropological. Now think of *how* the novel knows what it knows: not directly, not explicitly. 'Literature does not say that it knows something, but that it knows of something, that it knows about something,' where the term literature is understood to refer not to a 'body or a series of works, nor even a branch of commerce or teaching, but the complex graph of the traces of a practice, the practice of writing'. The consequences of this *of*, of this *about* – what Barthes also calls literature's 'precious indirection' – are that in addition to what is already known, literature can also tell us of what is not yet known, it can gesture toward further, *possible* areas of knowledge, to what is unsuspected, unidentified, unknown. The knowledge that is held and released, that is staged in and by a novel, for example – each one its own singular and variously detailed encyclopedia of the possible and the impossible – is therefore never complete or final. And yet, what literature knows *a great deal* about, what it knows very expansively and *the most* about (more, indeed, than any other discipline) is 'the great *mess* of language, upon which men work and which works upon them'. It knows about words, and of their flavour. It matters to Barthes that the French words for flavour (*saveur*) and for knowledge (*savoir*) should share the same Latin root.

He goes on: 'Curnonski [a celebrated writer on gastronomy] used to say that in cooking "things should have the taste of what they are". Where knowledge is concerned, things must, if they are to become what they are, what they have been, have that ingredient, the salt of words. It is this taste of words which makes knowledge profound, fecund.' Working with the taste of words – with how different words in different languages taste differently – the translator is dealing, always then, with knowledge, with the mess of different and potential knowledges of the world, upon which we work and act and which act and work upon us. In this sense, I realize, she is not altogether apart from – she hasn't delayed her involvement with – the world. On the contrary, the project of translating a book written by someone else, somewhere else, in a different language (*this* book *right now* over any other, never a neutral, but, as Lawrence Venuti puts it, always 'a very selective, densely motivated choice') is already and in and of itself a means, a close and detailed and practical means, to register, as well as a chance to renew, to vary the terms – the flavour – of her engagement with it.

I think of all the specialists whom Lowe-Porter is careful to thank in her brief translator's note: 'the number of scholars, authorities in the various special fields entered by *The Magic Mountain*'. The project of translation causing her to learn something more and new about lung disease, frocks made of silk, X-ray technology, philosophy, blankets, snow. I think also of Lydia Davis's ongoing translation diary, part of which is published as an alphabet of the problems encountered in the translation of Proust. The detail of the conversations her work led her to initiate: her 'correspondence with an old man in Oxford over the umbrels and titmice in the meadow outside his window'. Her debate with a 'horticulturalist friend over just what sort of ivy was turning colour in the Bois de Boulogne at the close of *Swann's Way*'. Katy Derbyshire researching the finely differentiated abbreviations used to refer to sex acts in the small ads, rewatching the TV series *Band of Gold* for vocabulary – all part of translating Clemens Meyer's *Bricks and Mortar*. My question about flowers and how plants and people die.

In November 1995 the scholar Timothy Buck published an article in the *Times Literary Supplement* – a shorter version of the arguments he would also publish elsewhere in the *Cambridge Companion to Thomas Mann* and the *Encyclopedia of Literary Translation into English*. It would be a devastating and, in the field of translation scholarship, now notorious indictment of the quality of Lowe-Porter's translations. Comparing a random sample of passages from *Buddenbrooks* in the original German with her English, Buck lists mistake after mistake after mistake. Errors of lexis, syntax and tense; unexplained omissions; unjustified rephrasings. At times, says Buck, Lowe-Porter seems like a bungling amateur, with a strikingly inadequate knowledge of the German language. Worse, an amateur with an inflated sense of her own importance – either wholly ignorant of or unwilling to accept her own limitations. Lowe-Porter was not Mann's chosen translator, Buck tells us. He had misgivings. He had wanted someone with better German. For *The Magic Mountain*, he specifically wanted a man – an absurd request, Buck concedes, but worth noting even so. (David Horton's more recent study of the English translations of Thomas Mann confirms that between March and June 1925 Thomas Mann had made concerted efforts to secure H. G. Scheffauer as the translator for *Der Zauberberg* – that is, to find himself 'a better instrument'; the American publisher, however, delighted by the success of Lowe-Porter's *Buddenbrooks* translation, disagreed.) Moreover, Buck goes on, not only was her German poor, look at her English: 'ungainly, unidiomatic, and at times incomprehensible'. She 'pressed' for the 'honour' of translating Mann; not relenting until 'the prize of being Mann's translator was hers'. She was 'hungry' for the fame that Buck seems to feel sure (that she felt sure) would come her way via the long-term association of her name with his. How could this have happened? Ultimately, the main complaint in this and Buck's other articles seems to come down to this: Was no one checking? Was no one in charge? How is it possible that the English Mann and, by implication, the whole great machine of literary history, should have been determined in this way – so contingently, so unthinkingly, by the vagaries of one woman's attachment, her presumption, her intellectual curiosity, her unfortunate and powerful writing desire?

When I was in my early twenties I worked as a part-time nanny for the family that lived around the corner: every weekday morning I'd get there at 7 a.m., wake the little boy up, get him dressed and breakfasted (his older sister could already do this for herself), walk them both to school and then, for the day, my job would be done. They lived on a street with a very sharp incline. Every morning the little one would race down the hill, zooming directly towards the road, while I'd call after him, terrified that today would be the day he'd fail to pull off his emergency curb-stop, for some reason incapable of persuading him to just walk with me, to simply hold my hand, while his sister, oblivious, stayed close to my elbow, updating me in her brilliant rambling way on the plot of the book she'd read the night before. Their mum was a French teacher in a secondary school, and as a student had been invited by one of her lecturers to do or collaborate on a translation: there was this text her lecturer was especially interested in, by a relatively unknown French critic. It might have been *Writing Degree Zero*, or possibly the opening essay to *Mythologies*. She didn't do it. She thought about it, but said no in the end. Though I can't remember the reason she gave, or even if there was one.

In a recent interview in the *Los Angeles Review of Books*, Gayatri Spivak, 'academic superstar' (as the interviewer describes her), recounts how she came to translate Jacques Derrida's *De la Grammatologie*. It was 1967, the book had just been published in France; she was twenty-five years old and an assistant professor at the University of Iowa. She didn't know Derrida at that time, nor anything at all about his work. She had been trying to keep herself intellectually clued in, she explains. And to that end would order whatever books from the catalogue that looked unusual enough for her to feel she should read them. She ordered Derrida's book, just published in French, and found it extraordinary. Her first thought, though, was not that she should do an English translation. She wanted to write a book – her own book – about it: a book in response to Derrida's. But then, she thought: 'Well, I'm a smart young foreign woman, and here's an unknown author. Nobody's going to give me a contract for a book on him, so why don't I try to translate him?' She had heard at a cocktail party that the University of Massachusetts Press were doing translations; she wrote to them and they said they'd give her a chance. It's really ridiculous, she laughs. But there it was.

In July 1918, André Gide went to Cambridge, in the company of his lover Marc Allégret, for a three-month stay. He carried with him a letter of introduction to Simon Bussy, a painter who made delicate compositions of the plants and animals he would sketch at the London Zoo. 'Among the chameleons, the owls and the parakeets, a few humans sat for him, too,' writes Jean Lambert in the introduction to the *Selected Letters of André Gide and Dorothy Bussy*, edited and translated by Richard Tedeschi. One was his wife: Dorothy, née Strachey, sister of Lytton and James. His portrait of her as a young woman hangs in the Ashmolean Museum in Oxford and is reproduced on the cover of the *Selected Letters*. It shows her seated deep in a gauzy armchair, looking out of the frame from behind her pince-nez. Her wrists are relaxed and loose, her hands half-open; she appears to be thinking. The wall behind her is this luminous pale, almost florescent pastel green. Lady Strachey had rented a house in Cambridge that summer, and her daughter, visiting from France, happened to be staying with her. Gide wanted to improve his English and Dorothy Bussy offered to give him lessons. In the middle of their lives – Gide was fifty years old, Bussy fifty-two – they became friends and correspondents, meeting rarely but writing often. Gide almost always writing to Bussy in French. '*Chère amie*,' is how he addressed her. '*Très chère amie.*' Bussy writing to Gide in English: 'Dear Gide,' is how she'd reply.

'Dearest Gide,'
'Dearest,'
'Dear and beloved,'
'Beloved Gide,'
'Beloved,'
Bussy was Gide's dear friend.
Gide was Bussy's dear friend, and the admired writer

she translated; as well as this, she loved him. She loved him, as Lambert describes it, with a passion that burned as ardently at the very end of her life as it did in those early years; she loved him in a relation, 'a meeting of equals', Lambert says, that was in this one sense unbalanced, because her love was clearly unrequited.

Following that chance summer meeting, Bussy became the main translator for Gide's works (in November of that same year, Gide wrote asking her to look over and if necessary to revise a translation that Lady Rothermere had made of his *Prometheus*: the publishers, Chatto & Windus, he said, were concerned that it was more '"literal" than ... good'). She would also write a novel, a love-story, the anonymously published *Olivia*. A 'little masterpiece', Gide would call it, when he came around to reading it.

In September 2007 I wrote an email to Columbia University Press. I'd read *The Neutral* – Rosalind Krauss's and Denis Hollier's translation of Barthes's middle lecture course, published in 2005 – and was wondering about *La préparation du roman*, the last one: did they have, might they be seeking a translator? The day before my email arrived their intended translator had confirmed his unavailability; I submitted a translation sample and (it's really ridiculous but) there it was.

When asked how she came to translate from the Italian, Ann Goldstein, translator of Elena Ferrante and Primo Levi among many others, often says some elegant variation on the same thing: it was an accident.

In 1927, Mann's preferred translator for *The Magic Mountain* either fell or jumped out of a window. Soon after that, David Horton reports, the publisher Alfred A. Knopf moved to confirm his agreement with Helen Lowe-Porter.

Following the publication of Buck's article in the *TLS* came a small rush of letters to the editor. Lawrence Venuti wrote in, strongly objecting to the 'typical academic condescension' toward translators and translation he detected in Buck's piece, defending Lowe-Porter's mistakes on the basis that standards for what makes a good translation change. There exists a tacit aesthetics of translation, he wrote; one that, like all aesthetic traditions, is necessarily of its time. David Luke, whose 1988 translation of Mann's 'Death in Venice' Buck had praised ('a model translation: faithful to the original, yet fluent') replied with new evidence of still more mistakes, and still more condescension. You can't blame Mann's complex sentences for this, he argued, or changing norms and standards. No, what we are dealing with here is 'failure'. Just look at her 'schoolboy howlers'!

Venuti came back with another letter; Luke replied again.

Eventually, Lowe-Porter's daughters wrote in, quoting a letter their late mother had once sent to her publisher, describing her own sense of her work.

I consider the letter, and the further lines from her correspondence that Buck quotes to build his case against her:

A perverse pleasure, she called it.

Offering its own experience of creative authorship.

Look to the whole, the letter asks.

And note the promise she lived by: she refused to send a translation to the publisher until she felt as though she had written the book herself.

I can see, with no German, but from reading Buck's article, that Lowe-Porter's translations contain many mistakes. (If you don't want to make mistakes, don't do translations, I was once told – an enabling dictum that I keep close to my heart.) I've since read Horton's recent, more generous assessment of her work and he, too, shows me that there are many mistakes. The fierceness of Buck's article speaks to the intense frustration, the profound sense of indignation provoked by what is considered a bad translation, with all its misleading, enduringly misleading, unfortunate, disastrous reading effects. I don't want to downplay this: the powerful and determining consequences of one person's translation decision, or sequence of decisions, or – in the absence of conscious decision-making – misreadings and omissions. The fierceness comes also, no doubt, from an awareness of how difficult it is to get a translation done, and how rare the opportunities can be, due to copyright, and funds and publishers' interests and circumstance, to get it done again. In a recent exasperated critical review of Spivak's *Of Grammatology* translation, newly published in an extensively revised version for a 40th anniversary edition, Geoffrey Bennington makes a case for what he calls 'the laborious and painstaking job' of translation. That is, for doing the work: for doing the thinking-work and the writing-work, for paying the attention that translating requires. There is no reason why asking for this, hoping for this, Bennington argues, should be conflated with policing (as Judith Butler suggests in her introduction to the new edition). He writes: 'doing the work and wanting the work to be done as well as it can be done are not, intrinsically, "police functions" at all, nor do they intrinsically constitute "quarrelling"'. A translation may always and from the outset be wrong, for the simple-complicated reason that the translator cannot simply present us with the original French, the right words in the right order – or not, at least, if she wants to write an English translation. But it can't follow from this, from what Derrida would call translation's 'principle of ruin,' that, as Bennington puts it, all translations 'are equivalently unsatisfactory, or that mistakes cannot often be identified and corrected'.

It has to be possible, in other words, for someone, for the critic, for the philosopher, for the harder-working translator, to identify and correct the translator's mistakes. Doing so can be a means of alerting readers to the fact of translation (to the fact of reading a work that has been twice-written; the second writing determined and motivated by its own history and context and agenda), and of preparing the ground for retranslation. It has to be possible to continue this inexhaustible work together: to query and vary each other's decisions, holding to or elaborating alternative measures of precision and care, without quarrelling, necessarily, or policing. And without shaming? This, it seems, is less clear. Bennington's article is titled 'Embarrassing Ourselves', a reference to one of Spivak's translation mistakes (mistranslating the verb *embarrasser* as 'to be embarrassed' in a given passage, when, as Bennington points out, Derrida's meaning is 'to be entangled in' or 'caught up by'). It's embarrassing that she should have made such a mistake in the first place, Bennington seems to be suggesting; it's embarrassing, also, for those who have trusted in her translation, who have quoted the sentences she mistranslated, building arguments around and on the basis of them; it's embarrassing – it's a shame – to be in the position of having to call her out on her many regrettable mistakes now. Perhaps embarrassment is simply what comes – what has to come – with the territory of claiming to have written a translation, with taking responsibility in this way for someone else's prose. If you don't want to risk being publicly embarrassed, then don't do (or at least don't publish your) translations. Is that right?

I don't know. I don't think so. It has to be possible to continue this work together, I agree. And I can see how this has to involve questioning and overturning each other's decisions, and the grounds upon which we made them. But I would insist on continuance over improvement: on doing this work in the name of continuance and variation over progress. Because the question is: are we really getting any *better* at translation, with our changing standards of practice? Are we all making progress? Is John E. Woods's newer translation of *Buddenbrooks*, published in 1993, for example, better than Lowe-Porter's? Not really, Buck concedes. For Woods, too, makes a number of comprehension mistakes. Is Woods's 1995 translation of *The Magic Mountain* an improvement on Lowe-Porter's? No, says Michael Wood, responding mildly to the fierceness of Buck's arguments (as they appeared rephrased in a chapter of the *Cambridge Companion to Thomas Mann*): 'Of course it's good to get things right, but I'm afraid we're all capable of careless errors at times. I have to say that I find the language of both Lowe-Porter and Woods lucid and serviceable.' ('Do we write better, do we read better, than we did 400 years ago?' asks Virginia Woolf in her broadcast on the radio. Do we translate better? What would it mean to claim that we do?)

What's more, there is something about the way the choice, in Buck's article especially, is being set out for me. Here is a choice: between, on the one hand and at long last, the promise of the *right*, the altogether better, and more appropriate translation of Mann's novel (made this time by the *right*, the altogether better, and more appropriate translator) and, on the other, the translator who happened to be there, who happened to pitch up to pitch for the translation commission and to do (some great quantity of) the work, the translator who was either spectacularly unaware or stubbornly unwilling to acknowledge her own limitations. Here is a choice, but it's not really a choice, is it? Because surely your choice has already been made. Who would want a bad translation? This is the further question that Buck's article seems to be asking, rhetorically. Who really, who rationally? Who actually on earth would want a faulty and mistaken translation? An overreached, miscalculated and ultimately failed translation? I react to this. A warm and instinctive reaction that no doubt has a great deal to do with my own translation experience, with the live memory of my efforts and failed efforts, and the beat of my own racing heart. My reaction is to say: well, I do. In this case, perhaps I do. I choose Lowe-Porter's version of *The Magic Mountain*. My precious copy with its creased cover. And I want to try taking seriously – I want to try embracing – the critiques that I hear levelled at her position and her work:

Would-be writer, which sounds on the first hearing like a position no one would want to claim, really. Until it occurs to me that the whole of Barthes's last lecture course is situated in this *would-be*: the lectures will tell the story, he says, of *celui qui veut écrire*, someone who wants to write – in his case a novel. The lectures will proceed *as if* this character, who happens in the lectures to go by the name of Roland Barthes, were writing a novel. In the context of a novel-writing project where the grounds for writing, the grounds for the very possibility of writing are never given in advance.

Amateur translator. Likewise, Barthes's longstanding investment in the amateur, in what he calls, in that lecture course, the practices and the values of the amateur.

Maker of wholes. Translator as writer or maker? And of what kind of whole?

Who refuses to let go of her translations until she feels she has written the books herself.

These, I realize, are the positions I am interested in; these are the terms that speak most directly to my own experience. I claim them. I claim them as the headings under and in relation to which I propose to think a bit further about the interest of the practice of translation.

Because there *are* deep pleasures in translating.

There is amateurishness, and not-knowing, improvisation and instruction, as well as the reach for specialist knowledge.

There is often a strong writing desire, great conscious audacity and difficult identification, somehow together with the more familiar humility and willing apprenticeship.

There is the making of a piece of writing: a new volume in a new context with very different materials.

And there is this close involving time spent with the sentence she is working on (then, the great sequence of sentences) that the translator is not wrong – or, I can't see how she is exactly wrong; in no way straightforwardly or eventually wrong – to feel that she has written herself.

WOULD-BE WRITER

Every Saturday morning I put on a pair of white and turquoise lady's trainers (*lady's*, I think, is exactly the right word) and head to an aerobics class. It is a new breed of class, and very popular: aerobics with a dance emphasis, which in practice means a large group of women aged between around twenty and sixty doing an energetic workout in a large gymnasium above a swimming pool in an unloved area of Paris. Mixing up the more obvious cardio moves with ballet steps, hip hop, Bollywood, tango. It is all very incongruous. It feels a bit silly. And possibly a bit suspect, our easy appropriation of these dance traditions, our simplifying and untroubled corrupting of these moves. But also, insofar as such a thing ever is: sort of innocent. What we do – brushing our shoulders off to outmoded RnB, agitating in sync to the deep tug of its deeper, spitty bass – often makes me laugh out loud. No one really greets each other, just the smallest of acknowledgements. Weekly, we come together and weekly we leave to get back to all the other parts of our lives. There is only one man in our mostly anonymous group. An American guy, a bit older than everyone else, in his mid-sixties, I think. He always wears white: white shorts and white socks, white singlet vest, white headband against white skin, white hair and white beard, all white and wiry and closely clipped like a goat. I know he's American because ever since David Bowie died he shouts 'Let's dance!' in the moments before we begin and my heart lifts and invariably people smile. It still takes me by surprise: the degree to which it's actually a joy, this being together, this moving in sequence together, even – somehow and perhaps especially – when we don't quite. When one of us persists in dancing to her own inner rhythm, half a beat behind or ahead of everyone else. It is beautiful, I think, how hot we get, how willing we are to get hot, to leap and to sweat, the wet we make making dark patterns in our improvised sportswear, picking out the lines of our spines, the hollows of our armpits, the deep vees in between our legs that we forget – in our absorption for a short while we forget – to feel self-conscious about. One morning towards the end of class, in the last five minutes or so when everyone is breathing hard, feeling relieved and quietly in the process of gathering themselves back in together after having collectively let something powerful out, I watched as the sunlight from one of the high windows hit and appeared to glance off the fingers of a woman three women in front of me as she stretched up into it, and I thought: I want to film this. I have never especially wanted to film anything in my life but right now I want to film this. Of course, I don't know how. I don't know the first thing about film- or video-making. But new technology makes amateur video-makers out of all of us. I had gone really quite far in my thinking of how I could do it, who I could enlist to help (whose better phone I could borrow), the permissions I'd have to ask, even the video-making artists I know whom I might ask for advice, before I came back to or rediscovered the thought that perhaps I could try writing it.

Not because, when it comes to writing, I know how.

I would go home, I think, and there I would probably open some of the books on my shelves. I would look, quite deliberately, at someone else's sentences – wholly unrelated sentences, relevant only insofar as they've managed to phrase, for me, some small bit of life. 'The coming day had thrust a long arm into the night.' I came across this line recently, closing a chapter of *Under the Net,* Iris Murdoch's first novel, which she published in 1954. A novel with a translator for a hero. Not a very heroic hero, it's true, or a very invested translator: it's all hack-work to him, the kind of derivative, unthinking thing a literary type might do to get by, en route to somewhere else. Translation becomes interesting in the novel only for a page or so, under the pressure of a conversation with a friend. A remarkable friend – the hero's one remarkable friend – whose philosophical position seems to me to approach Barthes's own, perhaps especially as it informs his book on photography. This friend – named Hugo – 'was interested in everything. And interested in the theory of everything, but in a peculiar way. Everything had a theory, and yet there was no master theory. I have never met a man more destitute than Hugo of anything which might be called a metaphysic or general *Weltanschauung*. It was rather perhaps that of each thing he met he wanted to know the nature – he seemed to approach this question in each instance with an absolute freshness of mind. The results were often astonishing. I remember a conversation which we had once about translating. Hugo knew nothing about translating, but when he learnt that I was a translator he wanted to know what it was like. I remember him going on and on, asking questions such as:

What do you mean when you say that you think the meaning in French?

How do you know you're thinking it in French?

If you see a picture in your mind how do you know it's a French picture?

Or is it that you say the French word to yourself?

What do you see when you see that the translation is exactly right?

Are you imagining what someone else would think, seeing it for the first time?

Or is it a kind of feeling?

What kind of feeling? Can't you describe it more closely?

And so on and so on, with a fantastic patience. This sometimes became very exasperating. What seemed to me to be the simplest utterance soon became, under the repeated pressure of Hugo's "You mean", a dark and confused saying of which I no longer myself knew the meaning. The activity of translating, which had seemed the plainest thing in the world, turned out to be an act so complex and extraordinary that it was puzzling to see how any human being could perform it. And yet at the same time Hugo's enquiries rarely failed to throw an extraordinary amount of light on whatever he concerned himself with. For Hugo each thing was astonishing, delightful, complicated and mysterious.'

'The coming day had thrust a long arm into the night,' so closes a chapter of Murdoch's novel following an epic night of drinking. Her translator-character Jake, clever and lazy, had been pub-crawling around the East End of London. So here is the dawn, I remember thinking to myself, as I marked down the page. Here is the dawn in a sentence. Here is the dawn, actually, as I have never seen it before. But as I *recognize* it nonetheless (with the new knowledge that the line seems to be somehow inaugurating in me). Here is the dawn, then, as I now wish to have made it appear. Here is the dawn *as I now might have wished to write it*. And here am I amazed all over again by what a sentence – the right words in the right order – can do. No to film- and video-making, then. That short fantasy-incursion into another medium served, in the end, only to confirm what I have known for some time, perhaps since childhood even: that when it comes to responding to, or registering in some way, the matter of life – dust-expanded sunlight glancing off a hot woman's fingers – I

want to see it written. That is, I want to try writing it myself. Why is this?

The question Why write? Why writing? Why do this rather than anything else? animates a whole section of Barthes's lecture course on the novel, on his turn to the novel, his newfound desire to break with previous, more theoretical, more fragmented writing practices, and to embark on a different journey, a novel-writing adventure. Why the novel? we might ask. And Barthes gives some explanation: because it is long. Because, unlike previously tested forms – the fragment, paragraph as discrete unit, the note – it has this continuity, this differently expanded, stretched ongoingness. ('While I may have often flirted with the novelistic,' he says, 'the novelistic is not the novel, and it is precisely this threshold that I wish to cross.') But before saying anything further about the novel as a form in particular – about *what* one might want to write, and even this way of phrasing the question is new since he had previously thought that 'to write' was an intransitive verb (but, as he says, I've changed my mind; I'm not immobile) – the first, more fundamental question has to be: Why, for him, and of all of his other life activities – piano-playing, painting, drawing, teaching – should it be writing, still, the dominant one? The professionalized one, since here he is professing to it: the Professor of Literary Semiology, newly appointed to the Collège de France? Why, even at this life-juncture, following the death of his beloved mother, marked by a powerfully felt desire for change, should the change be envisioned as a switch *within* rather than a break *from* writing? Really, the question is ludicrous, says Barthes. And unanswerable, because: How could I, or anyone know? How could I, or anyone, plunge down deep enough into the secret sources of our desires to figure it out? Ludicrous and unanswerable. But then again. Perhaps there is one answer. One general answer, one very spare answer, the one most likely to be the most broadly true of anyone who has experienced the desire to write. That answer would be: *I write because I have read*.

Recalling three scenes of reading:

Coming to the end of the summer holidays aged ten or eleven, and bored, having run out of things to do and read. My mum presenting me with a book that didn't look like a child's book, and so like nothing I'd tried reading before. A brown textured cover with no picture on it; very thin paper, a grown-up font. It looked plain and small and wholly uninviting. But I was bored, and the book turned out to be *Jane Eyre*.

French A-Level and it being announced that we were all going to be reading a novel. Which felt impossible, really: to read a whole novel in another language. We could imagine doing it, maybe, but only as a form of intensive reading labour: one resistant sentence after the other. It was hard for anyone to imagine actually enjoying it, getting caught up and transported by it. But then she gave us Gide's *La Symphonie pastorale*, and I can still hear Gertrude asking what white looks like, and why other animals don't – why only birds seem to sing?

On my year abroad now, and feeling very abroad I would often go to the top floor of the local Gibert Jeune: the English-language section, where you could buy Wordsworth Classics for one euro. I'd select some novel in the series solely on the basis of length. How thick was it, how many pages – how long might it keep me company for? *Pamela*! Or, better: *Clarissa*! Brilliant. Thank you: weeks and weeks and months and months (the perversity of reading in English while living the days in French. But then again: the novel as companionship).

Yes, but lots of people read. Many, many people read. It's true that countless people read, and take great pleasure in reading. There's even, Barthes notes, a bookshop in Paris called the Joy of Reading (or there used to be). Clearly not all readers are aspiring writers. And so the question asked in the lectures then becomes: Why not? Why aren't they? Why, asks Barthes, if reading is the prompt, the source, the wellspring for writing, are there not 'more would-be writers'? Why do the majority of readers appear to be contented with reading, to stop at reading (as I seem to be content to stop at looking or at listening – at painting, at video, at photography)? In other words: why doesn't every reader experience something like this impulse to *do it themselves*? Perhaps there are two kinds of reading and reader, says Barthes. In the introduction to her edited collection of his writings, Susan Sontag is excellent on Barthes's passion for typologies: notice how many of his arguments are launched by announcing 'that there are ... two ways in which myth might lend itself to history, two facets of Racinean eros, two musics, two ways to read La Rochefoucauld, two kinds of writers, two forms of his own interest in photographs'. Here, two types of reader based on two types of pleasure in reading:

The first is the reading of childhood and especially adolescence. 'The absolute pleasure of adolescent reading, immersed in a classic novel, the absolute satisfaction of reading, in exactly this sense that we read without wanting to do likewise.'

The second is 'the pleasure of reading that is already tormented by the desire to do the same, in other words by a lack'. From this second kind of reading, emerges what for Barthes is a broad, simple truth: I write because I have read.

Yes, but if reading is somehow and very often the cause of writing, Barthes goes on, arguing with the position he has just affirmed, it is not (it can't be) reading in general. It is not everyday, forgettable reading: the reading that passes us by, as William Gass puts it, like scenery seen from a train. He makes this clear: 'my Desire to write doesn't stem from reading as such but from certain readings in particular, local readings'. A handful of authors; and even then, just one or two of their books. For Barthes, it is Proust, but *In Search of Lost Time,* not the earlier *Jean Santeuil.* It is Tolstoy, absolutely. But *War and Peace* and not *Anna Karenina.* And even then, not the book in its entirety. Perhaps it's just one paragraph, just one resonant paragraph that sounds across a lifetime while the rest of the book falls quietly away. For Barthes, it is Chateaubriand's *Memoirs from Beyond the Grave* – but not all of it. A passage about heliotrope, a plant that turns its flowers and leaves to the sun, that is also quoted in *Time Regained*, vol. 6 of *In Search of Lost Time.* As part of the lecture delivered on 1 December 1979 he read it aloud. I quote it here in Andreas Mayor's and Terence Kilmartin's translation:

'I dined two or three times at the Governor's house, an officer full of kindness and good manners. He grew a few European vegetables on the hillside. After dinner, he showed me what he called his garden. A sweet and subtle scent of heliotrope was exhaled by a little patch of beans that were in flower; it was brought to us not by a breeze from our own country but by a wild Newfoundland wind, unrelated to that exiled plant, without sympathy of shared memory or pleasure. In this perfume, not breathed by beauty, not cleansed in her bosom, not scattered where she had walked, in this perfume of a changed sky and tillage and world there was all the diverse melancholy of regret and absence and youth.'

That's it, says Barthes. Just a short passage of text. I have no desire to explain it, he adds. There will be no *explication de texte*, no unpacking or explanatory unfolding of how and why it moves me. I didn't read it aloud because it contains some intellectual content that I will now try and make sense of. No, that's not it at all. If I chose to read it, it is because the text produces, in me, a sudden dazzle of language, it moves me in pleasure. I could say that it caresses me, and its caress produces its effects each time I read it. Even just now, when I read it out loud to you, I felt it again. We could call this *beauty* if you wanted to give it an objective name: this deep pleasure, this joy that Chateaubriand's language, his speech procures in me, that I receive like a kind of luminosity that is eternal and mysterious (in the sense that explaining it would never exhaust it). Like falling in love, like the joy of falling in love with one person in particular, among the thousand other possibilities, the thousand other possible texts, the thousand other possible faces. I'm well aware that the object of my desire, Chateaubriand's text, has come to adapt itself to my desire. There's no possibility of anyone else desiring it as I desire it. And there's the tragedy: I am, in all likelihood, the only one here to desire it with such intensity. In the same way as our loving desires get distributed. What I mean by this is: to fall in love is to choose among a thousand other possibilities – to choose someone who has adapted to my wholly individual desire, but in such a way that I have no knowledge of it until I meet the person who confirms that it has happened. And so it's a good thing, really, that desire should be shared out so very differently among different people. Because this is what gives us all a chance. Imagine: if we were all to fall in love with the same person! Likewise, with literature: some of us will fall in love with some texts and others with others... If we were all to only ever desire the same book, then what would be written would always be the same book, which is not the case.

The point is: we are not all moved by the same poetry or prose. We do not all feel with the same spurring intensity about the same poetry or prose.

'I like: salad, cinnamon, cheese, pimento, marzipan ... roses, peonies, lavender, champagne, loosely held political convictions ... realistic novels,' writes Barthes, famously, in a paragraph of a book titled *Roland Barthes*, translated by Richard Howard. 'I don't like: women in slacks, geraniums, strawberries, the harpsichord...'

'Who cares?' he asks, after writing this list of likes and dislikes out like a poem. None of this is of any consequence to anyone whatsoever. It is all apparently meaningless. And yet all this means – or, more literally – all that it wants to say is: *my body is not the same as yours*.

For me, for what it is worth –

the *for what it is worth* hoping somehow to temper the presumption that comes always underlying the *for me*, because: who cares, who really cares? And yet, all it wants to say is: I read with my body, I read and move to translate with my body, and my body is not the same as yours

– it's not Chateaubriand on melancholy, on adolescence, on this small patch of garden with its blue fragrant exiled flowers. Not really, not at all. For me, it's *Anna Karenina*, not *War and Peace*. It's Barthes's late work, the lectures especially. *My* Roland Barthes is not the early work, the mid-period structuralist, nor even the author of the three late, beautiful books – the experiment in auto-biography, on the lover's discourse, on photography. It's the writer of lecture and seminar notes, telegrammatic, elliptical notes, interspersed with stretches made from full sentences, small expanses of story and argument. Where there is this investment in the note as a distinct and provisional, rapid, mobile form; the bit of writing set down *for the record* even as it is invested in becoming-speech, intending its moment of public delivery, its circulation among the present bodies. And even then: it's really the last course on the novel, the slow preparation for and projection of a novel-to-come. It's this passage, for example, on these unique encounters that can happen in reading, once in a while in the lifetime of reading, like a face in a crowd, like a face to fall in love with in the crowd, like a line about an arm reaching into the night and summoning the dawn.

I know that not everyone feels the same way.

The theorist and Barthes scholar Jonathan Culler, who attended the Collège de France lectures in 1979-1980, has written of how disappointing he found them, how tiresome. 'Sufficiently so,' he writes, 'that I was very irregular in my attendance, preferring other Parisian intellectual activities of greater substance or theoretical interest – a choice which I of course deeply regretted after Barthes's tragic death cut short the course.'

'Translators are never, and should never be forced to be (or to think of themselves as), neutral, impersonal transferring devices. Translators' personal experiences – emotions, motivations, attitudes, associations – are not only allowable in the formation of a working [translation], they are indispensable,' wrote the Finnish to English translator and translation theorist Douglas Robinson in the early 1990s, one of eight precepts he sets forth as part of what he calls the translator's turn. Who would argue with this, he wonders? And yet it seems it is worth re-stating again and again. Not an impersonal transferring device, but a person – 'a holistic, gendered, literary being', as Michelle Woods recently put it in her brilliant study of Kafka's English language translators and translations – located in time and space, and always to a great degree determined, therefore, by her time and place, pressured and feeling.

'As for me, I should hardly dare call the feeling that I have for you profound,' wrote Dorothy Bussy to André Gide, in a letter dated 8 October 1919. Thinking back to their first meeting a year or so ago, the beginning of it all: 'How could it be, with no roots in the past and no hopes for the future? And faithful? Oh! That's a word I gave up using long years ago. But it's acute – it's sometimes even agonising ... And I have probably by all this forever destroyed what was pleasant between us – the "camaraderie" of the Cambridge days. Oh! happy Cambridge days, when I was just your dictionary and your grammar, convenient and helpful. And you had the same kind of friendly feeling for me that one has for a dictionary. I understood that perfectly. And you didn't notice – you were too much engrossed by other things – that your dictionary had eyes and a heart, was watching and wondering at you, was charmed and thrilled and shaken by you.'

An impersonal, impervious dictionary. Only in Bussy's image which now has (or had always had?) eyes and a heart, watching and wondering: charmed and thrilled and shaken (I can't read this without my own heart burning). She goes on:

'I couldn't help it Gide, I couldn't help it really. Aren't you the strangest and the loveliest and the most disturbing thing I have ever come across in my life?'

I have always wanted to.

I have always experienced the desire, the impulse to.

To find arguments for.

To argue around, out from, on the basis of.

My moods, my feelings, my impulses, my humours.

'*J'ai toujours eu envie d'argumenter mes humeurs,*' writes Barthes in *La Chambre claire*. A sentence-part translated by Richard Howard in *Camera Lucida* as: 'I have always wanted to remonstrate with my moods.' I want to argue with Howard here, conscious that my own translations would find such local scrutiny hard to bear. I am not sure that the thought invites the *with*, as if humours, moods were something Barthes wanted to talk himself out of or object to. I have always wanted – or felt? – to argue my moods, is what I'd venture he wrote, making the verb do all the work of disserting and elaborating out from. And then, continuing the sentence in Howard's translation: 'not to justify them; still less to fill the scene of the text with my individuality; but on the contrary to extend this individuality to a science of the subject, a science whose name is of little importance to me, provided it attains (as has not yet occurred) to a generality which neither reduces nor crushes me.'

This proposition: to start out from how things are for him, to speak out from his own subject position, of interest if only for the reason that we are, each of us, so wholly unrepresentative (Barthes, in his standing, his popularity by the mid-1970s, but also, by the time of the last lecture course, in his grief, as he mourned the death of his mother); not in order to remain there, on the small stage he may have now flooded with his own individual concerns, his list of likes and dislikes, but as a way of reaching toward our shared questions – all of this might be one way of getting at the broader project of Barthes's three lecture courses. I will lecture from here, Barthes tells us from the very beginning. I will induce outward from my own fantasies ('I sincerely believe that at the origin of teaching such as this we must always locate a fantasy, which can vary from year to year'): the fantasy of a small-scale community offering the ideal negotiation of inter-personal distance, of companionship and solitude; the fantasy of the neutral as a non-conflictual way of being in the world; and, in the last years, the fantasy of writing a novel that would finally speak of and for the ones you love. Let me tell you something, then. Let me tell you something that has happened to, or how things are, for me. Let me offer some sliver from life, from my fantasy life, as a place to start thinking together from. And in the telling it will become apparent – the hope, the risk, the wager is that it will become apparent – that just as there will be something to extrapolate, and so also to research, something to identify and investigate as being of likely concern and consequence to others as well as to me, there will also be a remainder: a leftover part, a residue in the circumstance or the detail or the phrasing or the something that is unglossable.

The effort to reach for the general in such a way as to neither reduce nor crush, in the hope that no one will feel reduced nor crushed, and so in such a way as to make no promise of a final theory, no totalizing claim with respect to the shared questions that the lecture courses were, nevertheless, deeply invested in asking was, for Barthes, a way of trying, 'in one's teaching, to attenuate the power and the arrogance of language; to analyse dogmatism, and to try not to practise it oneself,' which is how scholar and theoretician Lucy O'Meara puts it. In her discussion of this project, O'Meara points to a moment in the course on the Neutral, translated by Rosalind Krauss and Denis Hollier, where Barthes considers a range of strategies for offering what he calls 'beside-the-point' answers. Consider the formats of the roundtable, or the interview, he asks, and the kind of impossibly vast and grandiose questions that get asked there – the kinds of questions from which 'our social and political life is excessively woven'. Questions like:

'Is there a writing specific to women and a writing specific to men?'

'Do you think that the writer seeks the truth?'

The big universalizing question with its expectation of a big, universalizing answer.

Questions like: What is a translation?

And how to translate well?

What is a good translation?

I don't know. Actually, I don't know. If nothing else, I know that I can't answer for everyone. How to get out of it? (Gilles Deleuze on the interview, translated by Hugh Tomlinson and Barbara Habberjam: 'Most of the time, when someone asks me a question, even one which relates to me, I see that, strictly, I don't have anything to say.... Objections are even worse. Every time someone puts an objection to me, I want to say: OK, OK, let's go on to something else. It's the same when I'm asked a general question. The aim is not to answer questions, it's to get out, to get out of it.')

Imagine now, says Barthes, to questions such as these, big impossible questions demanding some generalizing authoritative response (a form of questioning which, in his grief, he experienced as a sequence of small attacks, a form of ongoing aggression), offering an answer that is entirely beside the point:

'The sky is blue like an orange.'

Or, 'I bought this shirt at Lanvin's.'

Or, let's say, if the question is put to you in public, standing up, taking off a shoe, putting it on your head, and leaving the room.

Writing from the first person is its own different – perhaps more moderate? more likely? – strategy of being always somewhere beside the point, of indirection. As Barthes will come to assert in the last course, 'I' is a *method*: part of a general effort to change what he calls 'the rhetorical conditions of the intellectual', to expand and vary of what it is possible to speak, and in what manner, in the hope of neither reducing nor crushing. I'd say, Barthes says, in the first lecture of the last lecture course, 'that I'm of a generation that has suffered too much from the censuring of the subject in the intellectual field ... And I would say' – insist? – 'better the illusions' – *les leurres* – the traps and illusions, 'of subjectivity than the impostures of objectivity'. So let me presume to tell you how things are for me.

The desire to write comes (is the feeling you get) from certain readings: the kind of reading that agitates you into making a trace of itself. Or to put it another way, and reaching a little further for an answer to his outrageous, unanswerable question, Barthes arrives at the following claim: 'to want to write is to want to rewrite', he says. And then: 'Every beautiful work, or even every work to make an impression, every impressive work, functions as a desired work, but I would say, and it's here that it starts to get interesting, that every work I read as desirable, even as I am desiring it, I experience as incomplete and somehow lost, because I didn't do it myself, and I have to in some way retrieve it by redoing it; in this way, to write is to want to rewrite: I want to add myself actively to that which is beautiful and that I lack; as we might put it with an old verb: that I require.'

There are sentences, half-lines, parts of pages that I happen across and find myself holding on and returning to because they produce in me something like a flash, a stun-gun of language, or what Barthes also calls, unapologetically, a moment of truth. 'The coming morning reaches its long arm into the night.' Yes. That's it. Here's the dawn. Yes. That's exactly it. Here's the truth of it as I have experienced it in life or: as life is now reconfigured to accommodate its truth. Here is life, as Barthes also puts it, but the point is: here is life 'phrased'. Here is life 'in the form of a sentence'. Yes. But that's not the *end* of it. There's also my hand. Or, I don't know, my legs. One of them beating fast time against the other. Already, my hand has moved. It's folding the corner of the page, reaching for a pencil to underline the line. I'm no longer looking at the page. I'm no longer even holding the book. I've raised my head now and my hand to my head and both hands clasped behind my up-tilted head and yet somehow I am still very much reading. 'Has it never happened, as you were reading a book,' asks Barthes, in an essay from 1970, which I quote in Howard's translation, 'that you kept stopping as you read, not because you weren't interested, but because you were: because of a flow of ideas, stimuli, associations? In a word, haven't you ever happened *to read while looking up from your book*?' The dance of readerly excitement: the smack of an open hand on a desk, abrupt shifts in position, breath quickening or slowing down. In these scenes of extraordinary encounter I recognize what Barthes describes as a lack. I am up out of my chair, or I'm not: I'm still seated, I'm folding down the corner of the page, underlining, typing the passage out, capturing it on my phone because even in its plenitude, even as it is right now filling me up, there is, I feel, something missing.

What is missing is me: my action, my further activity. These lines are not mine; I know that. The point is: *I didn't write them myself.* This can't be a general explanation of how all writing happens everywhere: there are other forces, other pressures, other motivations. But this is the proposition: that the lines producing the initial desire to write (what Barthes also calls 'the hope of writing') are those that, in their irreducible, unalterable, necessary power, invite, open themselves up to, make a stage for the collaboration – the audacious counteraction – of the active force that is me.

Actively adding yourself to an existing work can take a whole variety of forms – different in terms of their actions, their labour, their purpose, their degree of mediation – and in the lecture of 1 December 1979 he makes an inventory of some of them. One, no doubt the most obvious and the most identifiable, is copying: copying out by hand. People do this, says Barthes, or at least they once did. Once upon a time, readers would carefully fill whole books with their most loved poems. Now there's Twitter: a space for adding yourself actively to the lines you love: for retyping them, republishing them, circulating them among friends, siphoning off their authority, performing them as a part of a performance of yourself (investing them with your own subjectivity), as if they were, or to the extent that they begin to behave as if they were, authored by you, too.

Another is translation. Translation doesn't appear on Barthes's list. But I hear this talk of the desire to write as a desire for the focused ambition to write the thing itself, only this time by myself, as one possible version – as a very precise way of phrasing my own experience – of the impulse to translate. Translation conceived as a means of writing the other's work out with your own hands, in your own setting, your own time and in your own language with all the attention, thinking and searching, the testing and invention that the task requires. Translation as a laborious way of making the work present to yourself, of finding it again yourself, *for yourself*. Translation as a responsive and appropriative *practising* of an extant work at the level of the sentence, working it out: a *workout* on the basis of the desired work whose energy source is the inclusion of the new and different vitality that comes with and from me.

Elena Ferrante has written about the peculiar hubris of wanting to rewrite sentences that you didn't write. It seems in the first instance to be a matter of intensely felt identification. In an essay on reading *Madame Bovary* – an essay I read in Ann Goldstein's translation – Ferrante writes: 'I certainly saw myself in Berthe Bovary, Emma and Charles's daughter, and felt a jolt.' So not a caress, then, but something more painful, and this is important. A shock, a small sharp wound, possibly, like the snag of recognition that Barthes experiences when looking at certain photographs (That's it! That's exactly it!). Ferrante goes on: 'I knew that I had my eyes on a page' – she is aware of reading and not recalling – 'I could see the words clearly, yet it seemed to me that I had approached my mother just as Berthe tried to approach Emma, catching hold of her *par le bout, les rubans de son tablier* ("the ends of her apron strings").'

Ferrante quotes Flaubert in French throughout her essay, offering the English translation (which one, we're not sure) in brackets. She first read *Madame Bovary* at fourteen, she tells us: laboriously, in the original ('on the orders of a cold, brilliant teacher'). The fact of reading the novel in French matters because it compounds Ferrante's shock at finding her experience already written for her, but remarkably in another language, in the distant setting of a Normandy town: *'par le bout,'* writes Flaubert. *Par le bout, les rubans de son tablier.* 'By the end,' – the comma here marking a vital half-breath of pause – 'the strings' (the ribbons? they could be: Emma likes pretty things) 'of her apron'. But the original phrasing also matters because, if there is recognition and identification here, it is not only with Berthe, a character, the small, unwanted daughter, it is also with precisely this power to phrase, with the power of phrasing, forming *this* sentence rather than any other.

'All my life since [that first reading],' writes Ferrante, 'I've wondered whether my mother, at least once, with Emma's words precisely – the same terrible words – thought, looking at me, as Emma does with Berthe: "*C'est une chose étrange comme cette enfant est laide!*" ("It's strange how ugly this child is.") Ugly: to appear ugly to one's own mother. I have rarely read-heard a better conceived, better written, more unbearable sentence.'

The sentence about being grabbed by the apron strings recalled, for Ferrante, a scene from her own life; in the case of the sentence about the ugly child, on the other hand, it seems to be the other way around. Here the sentence seems to be producing life, occasioning it into being: here Ferrante is discovering her life by way of sentence, in the form of someone else's sentence, a line that she might have heard, 'that might as well have been' addressed to her, by her own mother, at least once.

Did her mother ever really say it? It's not clear; it doesn't matter.

'I have rarely read-heard a better conceived, better written, more unbearable sentence.' With that tiny hyphen, Ferrante brings reading and actually hearing, reading books and actually living, literature and life very close together. So very close, in fact, that the one could very easily get taken as seriously, and so pass, get mistaken for, or for a time swap places with the other. In this sense, Ferrante is reading like Emma Bovary, a character whose sensibility and manner of living (what the theorist and critic Marielle Macé might call her 'style' or 'stylistics of being') is directed by the sentences she finds in the novels she reads. In the most 'burning, devastating way', writes Barthes, Emma Bovary is 'formed, fashioned (remote-controlled) by the (literary) Sentence'.

C'est une chose étrange comme cette enfant est laide!

Ferrante affirms that she has rarely read-heard a better conceived, better written, more unbearable sentence. But who wrote it? Who did the work of writing, of originally phrasing what Ferrante hears-reads (or feels-reads, which my Italian friend tells me might be an alternative translation of the first verb in this coupling of verbs) as a line that may as well have been lifted from her life?

Ferrante's answer is complicated.

I did, she answers at first. The words entered and emerged from me: 'When I read a book, I never think of who has written it – it's as if I were doing it myself.'

Then: no, that can't be quite right.

It was, of course, Gustave Flaubert. 'In certain phases of my life,' she writes, 'I've imagined that only a man could conceive it, and only a man without children, a peevish Frenchman, a bear shut up in his house honing his complaints, a misogynist who thought of himself as both father and mother just because he had a niece. In other periods, I've believed, angrily, bitterly, that men who are masters of writing are able to have their female characters say what women truly think and say and live but do not dare write. Today, instead, I've returned to the beliefs of early adolescence. I think that authors are devoted, diligent scribes, who draw in black and white, following a more or less rigorous order of their own, but that the true writing, what counts, is the work of readers.' She goes on: 'It's my mother who thought, but in her language, *commè brutta chesta bambina* ("How ugly this child is"). And I believe that she thought it for the same reason Emma thinks it of Berthe. So I've tried, over the years, to take that sentence out of French and place it somewhere on a page of my own, write it myself to feel its weight, transport it into the language of my mother, attribute it to her, hear it in her mouth and see if it's a woman's phrase, if a female really could say it, if I've ever thought it of my daughters, if, in other words, it should be rejected and erased or accepted and elaborated, removed from the page of masculine French and transported into the language of female-daughter-mother.'

The path that Ferrante traces in her essay, from that first shock of feeling (the jolt, the pain of recognition, which prompts her to claim the sentence as her own) to then re-ascribing it, of course, to Flaubert, to this more recent and different effort of purposively writing out or retyping the words – that is, of materially writing out the sentence herself ('I've tried, over the years, to take that sentence out of French and place it somewhere on a page of my own, write it myself to feel its weight') – is also the path from adolescence to womanhood and writerhood. The point is, reading is its own work; it does its own extraordinary work. But it is not writing. It is not yet, not already, not *practically* writing. The difference between the first position (claiming the sentence as her own) and the most recent (trying to find a way of writing it herself) has to do with this shift: Ferrante's later-in-life feeling-reader has become a reader-writer. And in this instance she is, very specifically, a translator: Flaubert's sentence, should it ever appear on one of Ferrante's pages, will have been placed, rewritten, recalibrated by her, in Neapolitan dialect. *Laide*: the ugly end-word in French, set now like a stone in its middle: *brutta*.

Comm'è brutta chesta bambina!

124

Translation as a way of *practising* of an extant work at the level of the sentence: of working on and at it, of working it out – but practising for what exactly? And how might this relate to preparing?

The title of Barthes's last lecture course in French is *La préparation du roman*, and as the lectures progress the noun *préparation*, along with the preposition *de*, are invested with a range of possible meanings. Barthes speaks of preparation in terms of getting ready – yes: getting ready *for* writing. In his case, preparing for the novel. Working out and trying to establish what might be the conditions of possibility for a novel – or something like a novel, something of the order of a novel, something that one might be willing to call a novel – to be written today (in the late 1970s, when the form would appear to have already been exhausted – 'I know the novel is dead,' he is quoted as saying in an interview published in 1975). But, as it turns out, Barthes is less interested in the historical and social conditions of the novel than in the more particular and personal conditions that might enable a given writing subject, a given would-be writer (someone who wants to write) to actually manage to write one. A given subject such as himself, for whom the specific writing problem – as Barthes formulates it – is how to make the transition from writing short pieces, in fragments, and sort of discontinuously (from what he calls 'a taste for the short form') to writing something longer, more continuous and ongoing and sustained. The preparation of the title involves taking these personal conditions and capabilities into account: the would-be writer's fascinations and his failings (his limitations). For instance: the kind of novels I like most, says Barthes, at the beginning of the course, are novels of recollection, made from memory: Proust's *In Search of Lost Time*. But

I can immediately identify a certain constitutional weakness in me that would prevent me from writing a novel of this order. That weak organ is my memory, the faculty of remembering. I have no memory! he declares. What I am capable of writing will be determined, to some extent, by this, in the same way as the smallness of a person's hands makes it difficult for them to play the piano. If the novel of memory (made from memories) is unavailable to Barthes, then his novel will have to be made from the present. From what is happening right now, he says: under your eyes, beneath your nose. Hence the lecture course's great interest in the haiku, considered here as an exemplary form of noting (capturing, in writing) the most minute details of daily, concomitant life. If preparation involves preparing the grounds, the conditions of possibility for the novel, especially as they related to the disposition and constitution of the writing subject, it also involves gathering one's materials. For Barthes, preparing for the novel also means establishing what he calls a daily practice of notation, a mode of attending to and recording the detail of everyday life. These notes are what his projected novel will be made from. Preparing, then, in the way you might ready your ingredients before making a meal. Or – a different image which appears more than once in the course – in the way a dressmaker might lay out her different pieces of cloth in order to work out how best to stitch them together. In this manner, the preparation *for* the novel starts touching at and partaking in the preparation *of* the novel. In other words, preparing as a means of practising, exercising, learning – of readying oneself for the writing-to-still-come – and at the same time, preparing as already its own form of writing, as already taking the form of writing. Like translating, it is already massively invested in and takes the form of – it already *is* – writing.

126

For or *of*, then? The *de* in French allows for and suggests both. After wondering and wondering how to translate the title of the course, I eventually came to the conclusion that the second kind of preparation – preparing *for* – could be heard in or at least extrapolated from the preparing *of* the novel. That is, it seemed to me that 'The Preparation *of* the Novel' contained the possibility of 'The Preparation *for* the novel' but that this was not the case the other way around. I was also concerned that to translate the title as 'The Preparation *for* the Novel' would be to keep the projected, fantasized novel at bay somehow; to posit a clear distinction between that final projected outcome (an actual novel, actually written by Roland Barthes, which of course was ultimately never produced) and the labour of its preparation. When it felt – and still feels – important to hold on to the idea that Barthes's novel-writing was indeed already happening. When I wanted the title to make a space for the possibility that the late-in-life project for a novel was indeed in some way achieved – or, as Barthes puts it at one point, exhausted – by its preparation. A novel in the form of a public lecture course. This was my thinking.

But a question still remains: why 'Preparation' and not the more active 'Preparing'? Why not 'The Preparing of the Novel' or even, more simply, 'Preparing the Novel'?

Because, I thought to myself (although it's a question I have not stopped thinking about since): if what mattered was a verb rather than a noun (and a noun which names a concept as much as an activity; a new way of thinking about the practice of writing and coming-to-write in the form of a lived account of essaying it) would Barthes not have written *préparer*?

Préparer rather than *La préparation*?
Préparer le roman?

127

'*C'est une chose étrange comme cette enfant est laide!*' It's strange – it's a strange thing – how ugly this child is!

I imagine that for you, too, there must be a sentence. A paragraph. Or a longer part of someone else's work that you feel you know well. You like it. You love it, even. Or perhaps you don't. Perhaps it hurts you. But you are, nevertheless, for a complex of reasons, attached to it. Let's say that it acts upon you. You find that it acts and has acted upon you. But it would appear that you have already, also, acted upon it. It addresses you. Or is it that you have made it address you? And now you love or are wounded by it *because* it addresses you, because it looks, reads or sounds as if it were written *for you*. At some point in the process of becoming attached to the work you have misrepresented the work to yourself and now you have come to love your misrepresentation more, in a process of productive mis-attachment that the novelist Nicholson Baker makes into the hook of *U and I*, his extended love letter to the work of John Updike, written as a 32-year-old published but still a self-described 'beginning novelist'. There's this line in particular, writes Baker. This one line from somewhere: vast, dying sea. Baker deliberately chooses not to go back and reread the Updike novels he has read and loves, nor even to read for the first time those he hasn't yet. His project is explicitly unscholarly, anti-philological. It is to pay homage to Updike's works as they exist for him, to Updike's writings as Baker discovers himself in the act of thinking of them. As they are now lodged in his brain and his body and in the degree to which they have inspired and are continually inspiring (directing, fashioning, remotely controlling) his own writerly gestures. Among all the sentences Updike wrote, there is this one line, this small collection of lines. They might not be exactly what Updike wrote. This one – the vast, dying sea – is misheard, misread, misremembered. But it's a really good line. Arguably, it's now a better line. Certainly, it does something different.

'For the other's work to pass in me,' says Barthes, 'I have to define it as written for me and at the same time to deform it, to make it Other by force of love.' He offers a comparison: listening to the radio, France Musique, hearing by chance a Bach piece being played on the harpsichord. It is a movement that Barthes liked a lot, one that he would often play himself on his own piano, but more slowly. An amateur piano player, he would play it slowly, he says, for good reason. But as well as this, to his ear the movement was supposed to be sensual, lyrical, tender. And yet here it is on the radio being played *fast*. That is, three or four times *faster* (by the professional harpsichordist Blandine Verlet). So fast, in fact, that it takes Barthes a moment to even recognize it. The difference, he notes, was only one of tempo. But that was enough to cause something essential to be lost: the much-loved movement, now accelerated: all the characteristics he had come to associate with the piece had disappeared. They were *lost*, vanished, as if down a trapdoor. It's not that the professional musician was wrong, notes Barthes. On the contrary, historically speaking, her tempo was the right one. But the piece was no longer being played *for him*. He writes: 'The movement was being played in itself, but not for me: it had no meaning for me.' It was no longer the work he loved, the movement he had been playing, lovingly and mistakenly, to himself. And so, hearing it, nothing happened. Which is to say, 'nothing was created; nothing was transformed'.

'Let's dance!' shouts the goat-man. Or does he sing? He half-sings, half-shouts – emphatically. For me, before it was Bowie, in whose memory the Saturday morning exercisers now offer up our unlikely collective dance. Before it was Prince (it is still and will always be Prince), first it was Madonna. The *True Blue* album. With its Warholish cover: all pastels, all throat. It was, very specifically, the track with a violin intro: that long sequence of short downward strokes, the musicians in the video with their strangely angled heads, their furrowed concentration. When the violinists finally flourish it still gets me how all of a sudden there's the groove.

And unfolding now: the narrative.

A story that fascinated me as a nine- or ten-year-old, when full understanding was just beyond my reach: the mini-domestic drama of an unexpected pregnancy as told to a disapproving and disappointed but, it seems, ever-loving father. 'He said that he's going to marry me.'

'And we could raise a little fam-i-ly...'

To the chorus:

'Poppadum peach!' shouts my four-year-old from the next room, his mind full – or maybe not? – of the food his dad cooks for him, convinced of his righteous interpretation:

'Poppadum peach! I'm in trouble deep.'

'Popp-a-dum peach! Mmmm. Ooooh.'

That is genius, I think, listening through the wall. *My son, that is solid gold*.

kissthisguy.com, the archive of misheard song lyrics, had 118,399 entries on the day I was thus inspired to access it. Of its list of the hundred funniest, number two was Robert Palmer, *Addicted to Love*:

'You might as well face it you're a dick with a glove.'

Then a bit further down the list, Prince:

'I just wanna extradite your kids and – uh uh uh uh uh
– kiss!'

And Madonna again, *Into the Groove*:

'I'm tired of dancing in Obama's self.'

I have no way of knowing if these mondegreens –
that's the official word for them – work for you, whether
they work upon you in the way they work for and upon
me (they require some familiarity with late eighties pop
music). But they are good ones, honestly. They make me
laugh out loud.

I know that writing a translation is very different from copying or acting out a line from a book, not least because the translator, in my sense of her work, is a maker of wholes. It is different from misplaying Bach. I know that writing a translation is *very much not like* a four-year-old singing back to a Madonna track. Here is desire without responsibility, here are actions that make no promise of anything to anyone else, of making anything for anyone else, certainly not the promise of zero distortion (I don't think this is a promise that the translator makes – that any translator would ever make, actually – but it is often the strange expectation that gets weighted on her work). Desire, acting on desire, but without consequences, arguably. Like speaking in a dream. And yet still I want to insist on the common ground of enthusiasm that these activities (can sometimes) share. A spur which might also be framed as a curiosity, something like a personal experiment: to see what it might be like, what would happen, whether or not it is even possible for me to write this line, this work, in my own language, again. I don't see why situating translation in conversation with these other actions – copying, mis-singing, misplaying – should necessarily contravene the cautions, the particular attentions of translation in the narrow sense. Perhaps it's what invites them in. The translator knows that the work she is translating is not hers: she knows that it didn't originate with her; it is not something that she has already written or said. Indeed, she is not sure if she would be capable of writing or saying it herself, and perhaps this is precisely part of its appeal, of how it is appealing. Responding actively to its address is a way of opening her own writing up to its difference, its independence: to the instruction of its different energy, its unfamiliar thinking, its other rhythms. This, I think, is why so many writers translate,

134

or have translated, and speak of translation as a special kind of negotiation of the passage from reading to writing, as its own way into other forms of writing, as a way to move their writing elsewhere. In the lecture course on the novel, in a section on the way writers learn from one another, Barthes cites Julio Cortázar, English and French to Spanish translator of Defoe's *Robinson Crusoe*, of works by G. H. Chesterton and André Gide among many others: 'I would advise a young writer who is having difficulty writing – if it's friendly to offer advice – that he should stop writing for himself for a while and do translations, that he should translate good literature, and one day he will discover that he is writing with an ease he didn't have before.' I think also of a more recent interview with Javier Marías, novelist and English to Spanish translator (of Sterne, Nabokov, Conrad, Hardy and Stevenson among many others). When asked about teaching creative writing, Marías replied: 'I've not got involved with the creative writing industry, but if I ever had my own creative writing school I would only admit people who could translate. And I would make them do it over and over again.'

Too fast, says Barthes, of the Bach piece on the radio.

She's playing it too fast, he thinks.

Really, far too fast.

I find I am always quarrelling with the *tempo* of works, he says; whether or not I agree with an interpretation so often seems to hang on that.

In the lecture course titled *How to Live Together*, the fact that we can go too fast, or indeed too slow, for other people, for the person we are supposed to be accompanying, or is supposed to be keeping company with us, the person you are hoping will stay with you, your listener, your reader, the child you are trying to walk to school, is the central issue: the lecture course's crystallizing theme. A theme embodied by the sight of a mother glimpsed from Barthes's window, walking out of step with her son. Too fast. Dragging him along by the hand (so that he is forced to run to keep up). This fact and lived theme of what Barthes calls *disrhythmy*, and the power dynamics that are in play, and the disturbances it can cause. The question of the lectures, then, will be how to find a way of walking (being, living, also reading, writing and thinking) together that might somehow take account of our different rhythms, not through enforced synchronicity, but allowing for them: you read faster than I do, you get up earlier than I do, and eat later, you race ahead while I walk more slowly, and yet still (in this fantasy that Barthes is hoping to simulate in life) we'll find ways of coming together, points in the day for companionship, offsetting, modulating, interrupting our competing desire for solitude.

Too fast. And he doesn't like the harpsichord. Did he switch the radio off?

Too fast. Jen Hofer, poet, translator, and co-author of Antena's 'Manifesto for Ultratranslation': 'Translation stops me in my tracks. I might be going along (or in the case of how life feels lately, hurtling along) *como si nada* and then a word or phrase or image suddenly falters me, stumbling in my path, its body looming, an obstacle or blockage or snag or vortex that stops time and distends space *como si nadara en un agua espesa y borrosa*. A bang. Something inserts itself where it does not belong. That's the poem, the snag. The snag is a call to attention, a reminder not to take language – or anything – for granted.'

Too fast. The suggestion that written translations are (have sometimes been and are still now often) produced from a reader's felt relationship to a piece of writing, her enthusiasm for it – in the old sense of the word – that translation as a practice is a way for such a reader to add, attach, append herself (actively, ongoingly) to that writing by writing it herself and, in so doing, for her to change it, distort it precisely because what she has made is not *it* but something else (something new) that is now set in relation *to it* but might very well come to be read *as it*. The suggestion that mistakes can be productive, too, as well as regrettable, and are part of ensuring the diversity of literature, which in turn makes it difficult, perhaps, to decide once and for all what counts, really, as a mistake – say it all too fast and it gets lost.

It vanishes, like down a trapdoor.

Say it too fast and it sounds like a platitude: exactly the kind of reductive, crushing generality I want to try to avoid.

Books have their sources in, are made from readers (would-be writers) reading other people's books. Yes.

All books are made from other books and so, in their way, all books are translations in one way or another.

In fact all things are made from other things, and all things, and all people, have precedents, and so we are all translations – aren't we? – in one way or another.

Yes, okay.

No. Hold on.

Say it all too fast and we're already at some all-purpose consensus. (Because who, really, could dispute the fact that books come from other books, that we all, indeed, have precedents?) Say it too fast and then: What else is there to say? We – you, I – switch off.

A friend who translates academic articles for a living once listened very patiently to my account of how translation begins before saying: You know? For me, on the other hand. It is really not. Like that at all.

There are very obvious practical – physical, attentive – as well as intentional and political differences between the actions of copying for one's own purposes and translating, as well as between singing back – singing back and then holding inflexibly to one's own mishearing – and translating. Translation cannot dispense with – does it ever *simply* or *deliberately* dispense with? – the effort to get it right: a translation emerges in the relay between an existing sentence and the translator's first ventured rephrasing, the process involving a sometimes long drawn-out to and fro between what the translator might want to write and what the original sentence is instructing her to write, between what seems to work in English, and what the French is saying and doing, between a certain aesthetic of the sentence that the translator may well want to bring to bear on the French, her own ideas of what counts as a good idea, or good writing, and the sentence's own thinking, its own aesthetic, which is different, often very different, and serves as a repeated and necessary reminder – because it's true that in her quest for a sentence that works in English, for the phrasing of an idea that she is capable of thinking, she might be in danger of forgetting – that its difference is part of her motivation for undertaking to translate it in the first place. A to and fro, a relay: a venturing of something new on the very close basis of something that already and persistently exists. A new thing that is then sounded out loud in the new time and place of the translation before being set back into relation, repeatedly set back into relation and read and revised and reread against the original sentence and the translator's sense of *its* time and place, before being sounded out loud again, and again, and so on. It is in this space of close action, I think, that the translator begins to work out what on earth, what

140

really on earth, in this very particular case, *right* might possibly mean.

My friend's translation experience is an important corrective: having to translate fast, faster than she would like; having to translate articles that are hugely challenging intellectually, but that she doesn't have the time to get interested or invested in; accepting work that she doesn't care for at all; solicited by authors who require her skills only to quibble and dispute her decisions. It's true that translators commonly accept – or pitch for – commissions to translate books that they haven't yet read. Translators speak publicly of deliberately not reading the books they are in the process of translating so as to hold the adventure open, to keep it interesting, discovering the book in the process of translating it. What's more, translators translate works they don't like all the time. For the instruction of it, or for the broader sense of purpose (the world needs it), the opportunity, or indeed for the sums of money, the fragile livelihood of it. In an interview upon the publication of her new translation of *Madame Bovary*, Lydia Davis explains: 'I was asked to do the Flaubert, and it was hard to say no to another great book – so-called. I didn't actually like *Madame Bovary* ... I find what he does with the language really interesting; but I wouldn't say that I warm to it as a book ... And I like a heroine who thinks and feels ... well, I don't find Emma Bovary admirable or likeable – but Flaubert didn't either. I do a lot of things that people don't think a translator does. They think: "She loves *Madame Bovary*, she's read it three times in French, she's always wanted to translate it and she's urging publishers to do another translation, and she's done all the background reading..." but none of that is true.' They think: she 'loves *Madame Bovary*'. She must love it. Why else would she devote years to writing a new English translation of it – the nineteenth?

142

It is unhelpful, arguably, this insistence on sentiment, on emotion. What's more, it is a caricature: the translator as would-be writer. Like the caricature of the frustrated critic or editor: someone unhappily in service to literature, touching at its edges, jealous of its centre.

I too have translated articles by academics whose arguments don't concern me, press releases for art exhibitions that don't move me. I have translated the text for a suite of industrial clothing websites. I could tell you that they all had their moments of interest, actually, insofar as the puzzle of how to phrase a sentence – any kind of sentence – again in a new language is always to some degree fascinating, and productively taxing, in terms of the questions it produces, its invitation to think and make the contained – the productively constrained – writing task that it sets up:

Quelle que soit votre spécialité, vous préférez les habits professionnels extensibles, permettant une liberté de mouvement.

Whatever your speciality? your area of expertise might be? you prefer extendable professional garments, allowing freedom of movement. (Do you? Who am I addressing? Extendable? What exactly does that mean? Garments? Clothes?)

Which is something that Davis also says, in her recent inventory of the pleasures of translating. Pleasure no.2, she writes, 'is the pleasure of always solving a problem'. She writes: 'It is a word problem, an ingenious, complicated word problem that requires not only a good deal of craft but some art or artfulness in its solution. And yet the problem, however complicated, always retains some of the same appeal as those problems posed by much simpler or more intellectually limited word puzzles – a crossword, a Jumble, a code'. I could tell you all this as part of my project to insist – whatever my embrace of the position of would-be writer might otherwise suggest – that translation is not, in fact, a prelude to writing; a kind of fore- or under-writing, a preparing that is only ever on this side of where the real literary writing happens, but already and from the outset its own means of engaging

with and of doing it. I could tell you all this, with the conviction that I am telling the truth. But the point, of course,
and the source of my friend's eventual exasperation,
is that the stakes here, for the website, for the unloved
academic article, for the crossword are very different.
Very different to those that were in play when translating Barthes's lecture and seminar notes. For a number of
evident reasons: the visibility of the Barthes translations,
my attendant anxiety around getting it right, but also,
massively in the mix: my felt relation to his late work. I
know that a feeling for the work – responding to an appeal from the work, acting out this desire to want to write
it yourself – is not and cannot be the motivating spur for
all translators everywhere. The story I have been telling
pertains only to a small, privileged group. Let's call them
lady translators, irrespective of their gender: those translators apparently at liberty to pick their projects, to follow
their inclinations, thinking of Gide's Lady Rothermere,
making translations for her own amusement, where
the fact of her feeling for his work is clearly no guarantee (how could it be a guarantee?) of the quality of her
translations. It pertains only to those translators who are
materially enabled to spend their time writing literary
translations. The phrase is old-fashioned and unlikeable
and deeply condescending; I think it speaks directly to
the irreducible ambivalence of her (of my) position.

We need translations. We do, of course we do. The world needs them. And translation is work undertaken in response – in direct or indirect response – to that demand. But the nature of the work involved, the time that writing a translation takes, together with its lack of material support, its little pay and uneven appreciation, will inevitably narrow the pool of people actually capable of answering it. Translation is necessary, vital work. It is also deeply pleasurable and instructive and intensely time-consuming work. Approaching a kind of leisure activity, then, but one with its own precarious economy: its per-word fees (as if translating one word, one sequence of words, one book made of words, were ever equivalent to translating another); its occasional prizes. It is not my aim to celebrate these conditions, exactly; it's rather to recognize them in order for there to be a chance of varying them. As well as to point out – no doubt too fast – that even these conditions (these apparently ideal conditions? The lady translator translating what she loves, working from home, grateful for but not entirely reliant on what Helen Lowe-Porter calls 'the dribble of money', or otherwise secure enough to risk trying to make the various dribbles of money work) are complicated.

'You see,' wrote Helen Lowe-Porter, '... the job is to some extent an artist job, and I have always felt, with the more difficult books, that I should work over them without a thought of time-limit. But that is not the market or the publishing house view of translation. If it is not perfect then it is bad. I do not know how to deal with these blacks and whites, for my mind deals in delicate shades of grey. I simply can't afford to spend another six months on this job [the translation of Mann's *Faustus*], much as I should like to.'

I am a lady translator in my turquoise lady's trainers.

I am among the privileged and powerful: the taste-maker indulging in my tastes, my preferences, translating only the work I feel something for (or varying my projects: translating I am less interested in as a way of opening out the time to translate the work I feel something for, combining it with my other jobs, with an eye to my own instruction and desire for writing). I am the decisive, skewering and ideologically skewed interpreter, laying down in print once and for all (or until the next translation, which may well never come) what, in my terms, this sentence says, what it does; what, in my terms, this work says, what it does.

I am among the hidden masters of our culture, as Maurice Blanchot put it.

I am passed over and profoundly influential; my work is fascinating and derivative and determining and necessary and suspect. It is everywhere taken for granted and then every so often singled out to be piously congratulated. Or taken apart.

I think of Lowe-Porter, translating, as she puts it, 'in the intervals of rocking the cradle...'

She worked from home, supported by her professor husband.

A 'ten-year stint of eight hours of work each day on *Joseph*.'

She had three daughters.

What a privilege: to look after her children, while also doing the work she loved. Work that challenged her intellectually. Living a don's wife's life in Oxford, translating, writing out again, with her own hands and for years and years, the books that she admired.

But then – think about it: Can you imagine how difficult it must have been? A baby in the next room;

elsewhere, a toddler, and another older child: deep inside the project of remaking the sentences of *Der Zauberberg*.

But no, that's not exactly right either: she could afford a little maid, couldn't she? She paid her £40 a year.

What privilege.

What pleasure: gaining indirect – unwarranted? – access to and simulating, in the comfort of her own home, the gestures of creative authorship.

What thanklessness, though.

What misassigned, regrettable power.

What admirable dedication.

And willing self-effacement.

What quantity of mistakes.

What hubris.

What an extraordinary intellectual adventure.

All of it, all at once.

The story I am telling about my own impulse to translate is sentimental. And difficult, I know. In the way it lays claim to a certain kind of exclusive relation: *You do realize that I love this work*. As if that changes something. Because: Who cares? Who else really cares?

For translator Dorothy Bussy, translating was clearly a way of spending time with and feeling close to Gide. In a letter dated 27 May 1919 she writes: 'It makes me very happy to feel you are really pleased I should have translated the *Porte étroite* – I was afraid you wouldn't be. I felt I ought to have asked your leave before starting on a journey which was so clearly sacred ground, but I couldn't, because I didn't know till I got to the last page whether I should be able to finish it – I spent an odd winter with your book ... it was my companion. Day and night your voice, your sweet, excruciating voice, spoke to me. I ruminated your words, and their music and their meaning, and let them sink into me and become part of me – I hardly wanted more of you during the winter. But now that is over. I have nothing to do, and I am here – in Cambridge – without you – without a single hope of you.' But, as with my own translation relation, the reading and writing, the translating, the listening, the rumination over the length of their correspondence was all entirely on her side. With the exception, perhaps, of the three evenings Gide spent reading Bussy's novel *Olivia*: 'Yes,' he writes in Richard Tedeschi's translation, in a letter dated 15 January 1934, 'it was with a very keen emotion that I read Olivia's story, in the evening, by the fireside, alone in the large bedroom I have made my study ... And constantly, as I read, yours was the voice I heard.' Or, years later, on 23 June 1949, reading her annotated copy of Tacitus's *History*: 'the numerous indications jotted by you spur me on. I feel I am reading with you; your thought hardly leaves me. It's also with you that I am reading and rereading your translation of the *Nourritures* (the *Nouvelles nourritures* especially), endlessly astonished by your poetic ingenuity – and I feel I have not told you enough how grateful I am to you for having so well triumphed over the traps and pitfalls of that very difficult task.' For Éric Marty, writing on the correspondence in 1986, 'asymmetry' was the key feature of Gide and Bussy's relationship, and the reason why translation as a practice served not only as one of its drives, but also as its most apt and illustrative metaphor. Because, it's true, a translator may well feel deeply about a given piece of writing, she may have made friends with it, she may have made a short-term or lifelong companion out of it, she may have fallen in some straightforward or complicated way in love with it, but none of this will have any necessary bearing on whether she – or indeed her work – will be loved back.

The story I'm telling is sentimental, I realize, and not very new. See the Earl of Roscommon's 1684 'Essay on Translated Verse' (which I find quoted in Peter Cole's recent essay 'Making Sense in Translation: Towards an Ethics of the Art'), where the would-be translator is urged to 'examine how your humour is inclined' and then 'seek a poet [to translate] who your way does bend'. Which is all well and good, Cole writes: 'but what about needing or wanting to translate someone to whom your spirit or humour does *not incline*? Are there ethical and possibly artistic advantages in that?'

It is not very new. But it does offer one way of accounting for what otherwise looks like the strikingly haphazard history of literature in translation: a factor, along with all the other powerful and determining forces of economics, status, chance and circumstance, that works to determine what gets translated, and when, and by whom.

Helen Lowe-Porter: 'I cannot enter into the work of other writers unless their themes and techniques and general *Lebensauffassung* appeal to me ... And here, dare I say (aside from the dribble of money...) lies the reason I translated at all.'

Anita Raja, the prolific German to Italian translator of the work of Christa Wolf and Ingeborg Bachmann among others (whose lecture I read in Rebecca Falkoff's and Stiliana Milkova's translation): 'For thirty-five years I have had a secondary but constant side-job as a literary translator from German. I have translated – and continue to translate – essentially for pleasure. Since translation for me has never been a job to pay the bills, I have always been able to choose the texts that interest me, texts of good, even lofty, literary quality, texts requiring an intense involvement.'

And so, by extension, the whole great machine of literary history.

It is also the best explanation I can offer as to why, of the three lecture courses published by Seuil in the 2000s, Rosalind Krauss and Denis Hollier elected to translate the one titled *Le Neutre* into English over the others, leading to the middle course appearing in English first. Why I pitched to translate *La préparation du roman,* the last lecture course, over the earlier *Comment vivre ensemble.* Why the three lecture courses thus appeared, in translation, out of sequence, the second one first, then the last, then the first, determining the reading order for those readers receiving them for the first time (effecting a kind of *disrhythmy* or *disrhythmia* that was arguably not without its effects). Among all the other factors – timing, chance, availability, willingness, power, position, status – there was also this: preference, appeal, attachment. Unsystematic, and sometimes regrettable. Really ridiculous, maybe. But there it is. I like/I don't like.

I don't like translations, says Barthes. And indeed, other than the citation from Cortázar, translation as a practice is nowhere especially valued in his work.

I don't like to read translations of Kafka, he says, for example. I don't like them, however impressive my friend Marthe Robert's translations might be. It has to do with me, with my own writing activity: there's something unsatisfying about it; I take no pleasure in copying passages out. But copying passages from Chateaubriand, on the other hand, is a pleasure...

In an interview published on the occasion of the posthumously published *Mourning Diary*, Richard Howard narrates an early incident in his experience as Barthes's long-term translator. They had met when Barthes first visited New York – Barthes had a copy of the recently published *Mythologies* with him; they immediately liked each other and became friends. Howard translated a few of those short essays on myth, and then: 'I don't think he ever again read any of my translations. I don't think he had any ... it isn't that he didn't have interest. He would say that he didn't know English well enough to have it make any difference; it was just his satisfaction that they were in English. At the beginning I think there was some interest in that fact, but I never heard from him again on that subject. I would ask him questions. I remember calling him up once and saying that he had referred to somebody inadequately or incorrectly, as I just knew. Did he want me to silently correct the mistake? He said, "Oh, of course. Do whatever you want. I have no idea." And then there was some question of some king or even Egyptian pharaoh, and he said, "Well, make it up. Make it up. I don't remember the case myself. If it's not correct in the French text, just make up something." ... He was not an anxious author about his translations.'

'As a general rule, translations present a very serious obstacle to my reading,' says Barthes, in the context of a lecture on the haiku. 'Of course I can read the great foreign novels translated into French, like Tolstoy or Dostoevsky or Don Quixote, etc.' (All those novels? Yes, read them. I've read them. I have. Let me insist that I have read them.) But poetry is more difficult. 'It's very rare that a poetry translation is human to me,' he says. 'I have been reading some Valéry over the last few days and I found this note he made while in Prague, where he writes: "Lost abroad in an unknown language. Everyone understands one another and together are human. But not you, or you..."' Human, for Barthes, seems to mean this sense of including, of feeling included (addressed?), in contrast to the exclusion that finding yourself suddenly in the midst of an altogether foreign language can produce or represent (an experience which, incidentally, he savours when visiting Japan). Poetry in translation rarely feels human to me, he says. But somehow the haiku is this remarkable exception: a tiny poem, originally composed in a language he cannot understand, in a language very remote from his understanding (even with Czech, he says, I could probably make out a few words), appearing for him only in translation, and yet succeeding nevertheless in touching, concerning, enchanting him; the haiku, says Barthes, is human to me, *absolutely human*. How is this possible? It's a kind of miracle. And the whole first part of the lecture course on the novel is – provocatively? counterintuitively? – dedicated to exploring and speculating on how the haiku, as an exemplary notation of the present, produces its effects. How it produces its effects specifically and necessarily in French translation – since this is the form in which the poems are received – and on Barthes as a reader. '*My* haiku' is how he titles one of the sessions of the lecture course. To accompany his teaching, Barthes distributed a handout: sixty-three haiku in French translation, drawn from two collections, translated by two poet-translators: Maurice Coyaud and Roger Munier.

But as Nathalie Léger, the editor of the French edition of the lecture and seminar notes, observes in a footnote: where the sources of the haiku translations were not indicated, they were in fact Barthes's own. His own translations from the English – specifically, translations made on the basis of poems taken from a four-volume collection of Japanese-English translations. English: a language he read a bit, but didn't speak well ('Why is it that I have such little taste for foreign languages?' Barthes muses in his autobiography. 'The English learnt at school: David Copperfield, so boring etc.'). Why does this translation activity matter? Does it even?

In *U and I,* and thinking about how often, over the past thirteen years, he had discovered himself in the process of thinking of the work of John Updike ('constant summonings that were at the outset brought on more by sceptical ambition than by simple enjoyment, although the enjoyment and admiration were increasingly there as well') Nicholson Baker is reminded of the preface to Gilbert Murray's *Ancient Greek Literature,* where Murray describes his relation to that body of work. Baker quotes the beautiful passage in his book, making it speak to his one-way relation with Updike: 'for the past ten years at least, hardly a day has passed on which Greek poetry has not occupied a large part of my thoughts, hardly one deep or valuable emotion has come into my life which has not been caused, or interpreted, or bettered by Greek poetry'. A passage reminding me in turn of an email – a sentimental email – I once composed in French, a few years ago now, to Léger, following up on some questions she'd answered related to translating her edition of the lectures. An email about how often I find myself – discover myself in the act of – thinking of Barthes's lectures, and of the questions they ask. Questions about how to live, together and alone, about how to act in ways that cause no harm to anyone else, about reading and writing. Thinking especially, to my own surprise really (I had thought my interest was in the novel), of the lectures on the haiku. The haiku as an instance of notation. A means of capturing the present in its smallest – its most minute – details: buying peonies in June, for example, but still feeling the cold; an instance of life at odds with the weather. The haiku conceived as a written form which provisionally grounds even as it draws out these relations between the subject and the surrounding world. How it does so in this very minimal but nevertheless constitutive way:

suggesting, as Adrienne Ghaly has proposed, new ways of thinking relationality on a micro-scale; connecting, however fleetingly or long-lastingly, a body to the atmosphere, a body to an idea or to a line from a book and in this way, perhaps, to another reading and writing body, and doing so in a manner that is neither generalizing nor flattening, neither crushing nor reducing. How, in other words, inexhaustible the lectures feel to me.

Yes, I think Léger replied. I feel the same. I'd say they accompany me.

It is complicated, of course, Barthes's fascination for the haiku, and for Japanese culture more generally, as a number of commentators have pointed out. His fascination for the haiku he receives solely in translation. His claim on them: *my* haiku. This assertion: ohwowwowwow *it touches me*, and is – therefore? – *human*. The way translation is presented as a miracle, for the reason that just this once it doesn't present an obstacle to Barthes's reading, which in turn simplifies – and basically denies – both the labour and the powerfully motivated decision-making of the translators.

But when it comes to Barthes's own discreet translation activity, his unannounced haiku-translating activity, can I tell you, simply, that I enjoy it? I enjoy thinking of it: imagining this private engagement with a practice to which I know, or it seems clear, he was mostly indifferent. Did Roland Barthes ever write poetry? More specifically, did he ever try writing haiku? Did he ever try engaging, amateurishly, practically, with *writing* the poetic form he loved most? Here is an excerpt from the diary he kept in the summer of 1977 (dated 16 June; he quotes it aloud in the lectures):

De nouveau, après des jours bouchés, une matinée de beau temps, éclat et subtilité de l'atmosphère: une soie fraiche et lumineuse; ce moment vide (aucun signifié) produit une évidence: qu'il vaut la peine de vivre.

In Richard Howard's translation:

'Again, after overcast days, a fine morning: lustre and subtlety of the atmosphere: a cool, luminous silk. This blank moment (no meaning) produces the plenitude of an evidence: that it is worthwhile being alive.'

If I were a haiku-writer, Barthes adds, if I knew how to write haiku, that's still exactly what I'd want to say, but in a manner that's 'more essential, more indirect (less wordy)'.

Did Roland Barthes ever write poetry? No, no. No, I don't think so. I don't think any of the articles published in 'Roland Barthes and Poetry', a recent volume of the online journal *Barthes Studies*, refer to Barthes actually writing poetry.

Unless, of course: this counts.

Translating haiku in the context of and for the purposes of the lecture course, for the sake of others: putting the English haiku into French so that his audience could read and understand them, too.

But also and at the same time: translation as its own private writing experiment.

The project of translating like a weather simulator, like a little storm basin:

let me just see if I might be capable of re-effecting this minute event in language, somehow, the incident of it; like a leaf falling, writes Barthes, like a small fold;

let me see what I might make or fail to make happen right here and now, within this frame that the translation project offers, the conditions of new writing possibility that translation opens up;

let me see what might happen if I were to try writing these lines, these lines that I know I didn't write, *again* -

only this time *in my own language*

and only this time *myself*.

AND STILL NO RAIN / ROLAND
BARTHES RHYMES WITH

The handout that Barthes prepared for his students comprised of sixty-three haiku printed on the page. This mattered because – although he would be reading the poems out loud – as Barthes says, one must never underestimate the layout of a haiku: the space, the spacing, the way each one appears as a thing picked out, appealing to the eye, surrounded by white. A visual thing and at the same time a temporal thing, each poem effecting its own tiny movement, an unfolding over the extremely brief time of its reading. Here they are: sixty-three haiku on paper.

The handout was reproduced in Léger's French edition of the lecture course when it was published in 2003. As part of the project of translating her edition into English, I would have to translate the handout, too.

How, though?

How to translate this haphazardly collected collection of poems, originally written in Japanese, drawn from various sources, printed here in French translation?

In fact there is this one book of haiku in particular, says Barthes, in the lecture delivered on 6 January 1979. It's very important to me but: I've lost my copy of it. I've tried to buy the book again, but it no longer seems to be sold anywhere. I went to the library to find it – to a research library, the Bibliothèque nationale on the rue de Richelieu. But found it impossible to locate the bibliographical reference for a book that I once held in my hands. I did once hold it in my hands, he says, so it can't be a hallucinated object. This book, he asks his audience: if you happen to find the reference, could you please pass it on to me – so I can share it with everyone else here? It's a very complete collection of haiku in English, in four volumes.

If you find the reference, could you give it to me?

And if you happen to come across the book, could you buy it?

Please, and I'll buy it back from you?

In 2008 I looked for and found the volumes Barthes was referring to – very easily now, because Léger supplies the full bibliographical details in her editor's notes. And because there is now a copy in the national library, at its second site on the Avenue de France. I spent the last weeks of the summer in the library with Spring, Summer-Autumn, and Autumn-Winter, published between 1949 and 1952 and edited and translated by R. H. Blyth. They are thick books with pale, watery covers: a bird on a branch, perching next to a japonica blossom the size of its small head; a softly yellowing tree; a man and his donkey walking through the snow. I was looking through them for the thirty or so haiku that Barthes had picked out from those pages and translated into French. Thirty or so little poems, tiny incidents of language, working from Barthes's French translations and trying to guess back at and in this way to locate the 'original' poems in Blyth's English. Here is a Barthes translation:

> Si rudement tombe
> sur les oeillets
> l'averse d'été

Oeillets. Paging through Summer-Autumn looking for 'carnations', I reached the end.

I had – I must have – missed them.

I am skimming not reading, I told myself.

Clearly not doing this attentively enough, slowly enough. Thinking of other things, probably of September, and what will happen then. No carnations.

Summer rain?

I'll look instead for 'summer rain'.

Surely the back-translation of *averse d'été*.

No? So how did you arrive at *averse*?

Could you tell me? Please. I'm a bit tired now. By what effort of the imagination am I supposed to think my way – from my new and distant setting, touching at your French translations – to reach, in these English pages, wherever you were then?

I was once asked, at the time of publishing and publicly presenting my translations, whether I had ever felt excluded from Barthes's fantasies. The fantasy, for example, of living-together, as it manifests in the monasteries of Mount Athos: small, exclusively male communities; eight to ten men, finding a rhythm for their lives between separate rooms for sleeping and a common space for coming together, for prayer and eating. I was very struck by this. Excluded? Was I missing something? Or, rather, was the suggestion that I had clearly been missing something? Perhaps what D. A. Miller, in his beautiful *Bringing out Roland Barthes*, calls the 'discreet but discernible gay specificity of Barthes's text'? The erotics of proximity and distance, let's say, as Barthes reads them in the texts of Saint Benedict, the codes around who could sleep between whom, who might have an excuse to touch whom. Had passages like this not always been, for me, *all part of it*? I took the question sensitively, I remember, as a public reminder of my difference. And so as an indirect querying of my identification with Barthes's late work: my claim to having a relationship with it, to feeling addressed by and included in it. All of which, in the bright glare of the question, was now starting to look a bit improbable, perhaps; a bit inappropriate. I think I said something about the fantasy of the dressmaker, the seamstress who features in the lectures on the novel. The dressmaker who goes from house to house, gleaning bits of life, bits and pieces of life, collecting her materials before returning to her home to work on them, working them up, piecing them together: the dressmaker like the novelist. I pointed to her, I think. Offering her activity, or at least Barthes's fantasized version of her activity (blurring and softening the edges of what must have been the reality of it), as one that I – with my domestic translation practice – might more legitimately claim to identify with. But the question and my on-the-spot answer – these are things I've thought a lot about since.

And on reflection I would answer differently now. I would argue that this is what reading offers us: occasions for inappropriate, improbable identification. For powerful reality-suspending identification with a character, a writer, an idea, an experience, a fantasy. Fantasies that apparently have nothing to do with me – isn't this, in its way, the power of a fantasy? – that do not appear to directly concern or pertain to me. But that catch me up nonetheless. Like a complicated miracle. Like the everyday complicated miracle of reading books written by other people – especially, perhaps, books in translation, originally written in languages we will never speak, about places we will never visit and experiences we will never have. Books that, through the work of translators, address us nevertheless, include us in the remit of their address (not by expanding it, necessarily, to some broad and flattened out universal of shared experience but, as in the haiku, by narrowing it and sharpening it to the absolutely local, the absolutely particular). I would say – in the light of the question – that I was only just now registering how private my experience of that address had been. Working more or less silently at home on the translations, in the quiet of a reading-writing relationship developed over a couple of years, hearing it for the most part in my head. It was strange to speak of it out loud, I'd say. Very aware, now, and not really needing it to be pointed out, of the kind of speech-producing body I have. Holding the floor for a bit longer, I'd say something about my body's capacity to make sound: my keen awareness of the muscles in my mouth and the stress-rhythms of the language I grew up in. I would describe how, when I first moved to Paris, I worked as a language assistant teaching English phonetics at a university in the suburbs. How, as part of the standard pedagogy, a funny thing – funny at the time, and funnier as I think of it now – the first task of the year was always to have the students recite Humpty Dumpty.

It was an exercise in intonation, a workshop in sing-song:

Humpt-y *dumpt*-y *sat* on a *wall* is what I'd have them say.

Humpt-y, dumpt-y *sat* on a *wall*.

(*Where* did he *sit*? He

sat on a *wall*)

The students would laugh at me, disbelievingly: *Non mais vraiment, Madame, vous rigolez!* Surely you don't – not really, not in real life, not in everyday real life – speak that way, do you? Come on, does anyone?

I do! I'd say (it was part of my job to insist on the weird value of simulating Received Pronunciation). But it was also, interestingly, true:

In *En*glish, in *Eng*-land, we *do-o*!

We start low, we go high, we sink again, we *em-pha-size*.

We do! Honestly, I'd say: we *doooo*.

But I know that in French you don't. I know that when I speak your language I bring the inflections. I make it rise and fall in ways that even *I* can hear are quite unnatural to it. I do this without thinking and instantly it marks me out. You're not French are you? No, you're right, I'm English. Half a sentence and already you've placed me: in a body with a mouth that can't help adding this peculiar signature as it speaks.

So much for stress-rhythm, though, what about the vowels?

Like the vowel in Barthes. I have sometimes tried practising saying the name Roland Barthes out loud on my own at home. In preparation for speaking of his work and my translator's relationship to his work before an audience, any audience – by which I mean simply the audience that is other people:

Bah! That's how I know it should go, having listened to friends, to colleagues say his name (there's even a website for this: pronounceitright.com). Or at least that's how it should start. A quick burst of sound.

Bah! A short tight but still rising vowel. Ba-AH – leading into the high r. Reaching for it up in the roof of my mouth. Then rolling it. Attempting now to roll it: chin tilted slightly to the ceiling, a high quick scouring: Bah-AHRR- before ending abruptly and cutting off all sound on the *tuh*.

Barthes.

This is silly, I know: it's humiliating, really. I can't do it; I find I can never do it without some great self-conscious effort.

But surely, I tell myself, it doesn't matter. I mean, who cares? Who really cares?

(Perhaps I could do what I want.

Could I? I could just make something up...)

Surely it doesn't *really* matter that when alone and left to my own devices, in the reading solitude in which this sense of a relation was formed in the first place, and with the inner voice that I use to speak silently to myself, a voice that sounds quite a lot like the one I use when speaking out loud: higher and reedier than I'd like, with long south-of-England vowels – in *that* voice, in *my* mouth:

Roland Barthes rhymes with
art
(with /aːt/)

It does though, doesn't it? Is what I'd end up saying, in my late imagined response, my *esprit d'escalier*, my 'staircase wit', as the dictionary has it (its funny, awkward translation, but then: how else to do it?), inviting the questioner to agree with me. Clearly, it matters how we say each other's names: those proper nouns – the names of people and sometimes of places – that we don't translate, that we no longer tend to translate, but instead let pass apparently untouched from language into language. Names like Hans Castorp, like *Tous-les-Deux*. Although not exactly like Robinson Crusoe, whom in the lectures Barthes calls, casually, Robinson, as if he were a friend. How we say these names is one of the ways we display and lay claim to familiarity, to intimacy, to a specialist knowledge of each other, and of each other's work. Who has not felt a bit of humiliation, a small flush of shame, when speaking out loud, at the realization that the name you'd thought you had a handle on pronouncing is in fact – according to some authority, some consensus, a more knowledgeable other – pronounced differently? Who has not used a private name, a pet name coined for a lover or a friend or a child out in public, as a covert but highly effective tactic, a way of announcing your relationship, making it clear to everyone around you who you are to each other, making the channel of familiar communication between the two of you suddenly appear to others, in a way that briefly blocks those others out, leaving the rest of us now scrambling to reimagine and reconfigure our relationships to you both? How we say each other's names out loud is one of the ways in which we position ourselves, publicly, in relation to each other, to other people, to languages, to cultures, to knowledge, and to power – consciously as well as inadvertently. It's how we intimidate each other, patronize each other, how we surreptitiously deny each other the right to speak. It's also how we approach each other, show affection, show our care and our love. It's how we get close and bear witness to our closeness, our long-term or short-lived bonds. It's how we create these relations, one-directional, or reciprocal, passing names like warm pebbles amongst ourselves. It's how we work out who we will have conversations with, how we decide who we can and who we want to talk to.

It does matter, is what I would say, in the end. I realize this. I took your query, sensitively, to be about who I am, about who on earth I think I am (to be identifying, to be claiming to *identify*, with this work, with its queer fantasy scenarios, its late-in-life urgency and grief, its novel-writing projects, its ideas about reading and writing). And perhaps you're thinking: is this closeness then?

Is this what closeness looks like?

The lady translator, shouting vowels at her ceiling in preparation for speaking out loud, out of a concern to protect her reading relationship, to not have it publicly queried and thereby taken away from her. Out of an anxiety that the audience might very well find grounds to question her claim to familiarity, her sense of being spoken to by that work, from the instant they hear her speak, or fail to speak, of it.

To speak, that is, of the late work of a critic, theorist and writer whose very last piece of writing, the one that was left on his desk on the day of the accident that led to his death, was titled: 'One Always Fails in Speaking of What One Loves.'

Or, in an alternative translation: we always fail to speak of what we love.

Or alternatively again: you (a general you that includes me, the you we use in English, sometimes, to embrace both you and me),

you always fail to speak, when you speak of what you love.

'Attention!' says Barthes at key moments in the last lecture course. In French, he says: 'Attention!' Take notice, take care, be careful, hold on.

It's a note of caution that he is careful to sound – that he repeatedly sounds – whenever he finds himself directly relating his own novel-writing project to the lives and works of the writers he admires (Dante, Flaubert, Tolstoy, Proust, Kafka...). It goes like this: 'Attention! when I speak of these writer-heroes, *I am identifying-with, not comparing-myself-to.*' There is a difference, insists Barthes: 'the great writer, like Dante, is not someone to whom one can compare oneself, but whom one can, and one wants to, more or less partially, identify with. (I don't have the right to compare myself with Dante but I have the right to identify with him.)' The right to identify-with without risking the presumptuousness of comparing-oneself-to: is this not one of the basic freedoms of reading? The right to identify-with: with Barthes, for example. But also, and perhaps more closely still, with Helen Lowe-Porter, with Dorothy Bussy, with these extraordinary women translators whose stories I am so interested in, whose positions and feelings I want to understand in order to better understand my own.

Yes, I think so.

But then again, the more I think about it the more I wonder whether it is indeed identification that I feel: whether what I have termed closeness has *identification* at its source. Might it not more simply have to do with repeatedly-wanting-to-spend-time-with? With the long-term company I want to keep: something like a desire for *this* companionship in particular. I would rather read Barthes than a great many other writers. I shelve and pile his books near me. Why? Not because I find myself and my own experience in his work, always or even often, but for the reason that I don't.

'It's not true that the more you love, the better you understand,' writes Barthes in *A Lover's Discourse*, translated by Richard Howard, under the heading 'The Unknowable'. '[A]ll that the action of love obtains from me is this wisdom.' Then, in the next paragraph: 'Or again, instead of trying to define the other ("What is he?"), I turn to myself: "What do I want, wanting to know you?" What would happen if I decided to define you as a force and not a person? And I were to situate myself as another force confronting yours?'

I'm not sure it's true that I *identify* with Lowe-Porter, the professor's wife, with her 'little art', her translator's notes, so over-the-top in their self-deprecation, so very excessive in their humility (thanking the scholars, the 'authorities in the various special fields entered by *The Magic Mountain*', she goes on to write: 'without whose help the version in all humility offered here to English readers, lame as it is, must have been more lacking still'). Likewise, do I identify with Bussy, with everything she says about translating in her correspondence? Or is it more that this is the body of writing, these are particular ideas and positions that I choose – that for the moment I am choosing – to be with: to think and argue and write with and against. These are the forces that I am drawing on and confronting with my own, getting sometimes bewildered by and uncomprehending. Lydia Davis has written about taking pleasure in the company afforded – the energy that is tapped – by the work of translation. In her inventory of the pleasures of translating, pleasure no. 4 is all about not thinking or writing alone. She writes: 'When you are translating, you are working in partnership with the author; you are not as alone as you are when writing your own work. You sense the author's hovering presence, you feel an alliance with him, and a loyalty to him, with all his good and his less good character traits, whether he is neurotic and difficult, and at the same time generous and funny, like Proust, or tender toward his family and at the same time full of contempt for a great many people and types of people, like Flaubert. Perhaps it is that you overlook his less admirable qualities in admiration for what he has written; or your judgment of him is tempered by your awareness that you have a degree of power over his work – to do well or ill by him in the small arena of the translation.'

In the lecture delivered on 13 January 1979 – a week after worrying over its loss, Barthes announces the good news: the sought-after book has been found. Some unknown persons have been kind enough to find the book for me as well as the reference and they managed to do so exactly one hour after me speaking of it here, he says, which is prodigious for an unfindable book. So: thank you. Here's the reference: it's by an Englishman named Blyth (he adds: I'm not sure if I'm pronouncing that correctly), first name: Reginald Horace. Title: *A History of Haiku*. Thank you. Thank you all for your help.

In the library, meanwhile, late in the summer – a hot summer, and a new effort.

(Could I not just make it up? Just do what I want and make something up?)

I paged through the book again, feeling that I really should find the 'original' poem in English, but without any clear idea of what to do with it should I find it. Copy out Blyth's translation and offer it to readers of the lectures in English – as the 'original' poem, the original translation that Barthes once read and selected to translate into French? Perhaps that would make the most sense.

But there are no carnations here.

And still no rain – not even any rain.

I closed the book hard. Left the desk to do a short tour of the reading room. Remonstrated with myself and returned. I sat down heavily and let the book fall open. And then, of course, all of a sudden it was there:

The summer shower
falls on the pinks
so roughly

Ha! Feeling triumphant now!
Ha! *Ha!* (Rhymes with *Bah!*)
Then, aware of the readers and researchers around me raising their heads in alarm, under my breath and to no one in particular:
So, no carnations, then.
At no time carnations. Pinks. *Pinks!*
And no rain. Of course no rain. A *shower.*
That abrupt and heavy falling.
On the frilly flowers. So *roughly.*

One small poem found. But there were thirty or so more to go and a decision still to make. Should I offer the English exactly as it is here, in Blyth's translation? Blyth, after all, 'was a brilliant translator' according to Adrian James Pinnington. A proponent of what Pinnington calls the 'minimalist' approach: translating the haiku 'as literally as possible', even abbreviating it, while at the same time bringing his translations 'at times close to a kind of concrete poetry'.

But the sequence of Barthes's translation is entirely different from Blyth's. He has inverted it: in his poem, the roughly falling comes first (*si rudement tombe*), then the pinks (*sur les oeillets*), and only then the summer shower (*l'averse d'été*).

Would it not be better, then, to work the difference of Barthes's decisions back into the English? As a way of registering the touch of his hands, his reading and thinking, the further process that the poems were put through, his own local writing out of them, as part of the thinking, the argument, which this printed-out selection of poems was intended to illustrate?

In its attention to detail, taking note of the smallest differences, the haiku, says Barthes, makes these very fine distinctions. Haiku-writing is conceived in the lectures as an effort of dividing the real: of making ever finer, ever subtler divisions and distinctions within the real. Pinks, then, as discretely quite different from carnations. (I find an article on the internet by Caroline Whetman titled 'A UK view of Pinks vs. Carnations': as well the genetic variance, I learn, the former are so much older: 'Their history is impressive, having been cultivated for hundreds of years with much evidence of wild forms abounding on the mountains, hills and valleys of ancient Greece.') Pinks, not carnations. The quality of this rain. The times of the day: from one minute to the next and the way the light changes. It is possible, says Barthes, to go on dividing like this forever. Like the physicists, whose work is to make these ever tinier and ever finer divisions in matter (descending infinitely, or almost infinitely: infinite divisibility). But with the difference that the writer of haiku must at some point stop. At some given moment in the making of these ever more subtle distinctions, the haiku-writer – or rather the poem he makes – says: I have set down language, I have stopped language; I have set it down in the sense of deposited it. To deposit: to put down or place in a specific place, sometimes for safe-keeping; also, (of water, the wind, or other natural agency) to lay down (matter) gradually as a layer or covering). When I reached the rough manner of this rain, the scrunched petals of these flowers, their fraying edges, I stopped and set down language. *At this given moment* in the ever more subtle, potentially infinite, shading of differences among things, the process was (provisionally) stopped.

Which pertains, I think, to translating: the worry worry worry over the difference between this word and that, the weight and angle and sound and even the taste of this word over that; the divisions of the real this effects and the degree to which these overlap with or fail to overlap with the divisions I sense in French. And the point at which it has to stop. A decision has to be made. Language is set down. Reminding me of a different image from the same lecture course, one that comes much later, long after the first half on the haiku. Where the question, now, is how to move from an Imaginary of writing, a fantasy of the novel (which is of the order of the potential, the preparatory, and so the potentially infinite) to the actuality of writing one (which is of the order of a decision, a sequence of decisions, and the material setting down of language). Barthes offers another image of feminized labour, but not the dressmaker this time, instead: the novel-writer as *stoppeuse*. In a lecture delivered on 2 February 1980, he says this: when I was a child, I would see around me – it's a very familiar image from my childhood, especially since I had a childhood surrounded by women, my grandmother, my aunt, my mother – women obsessed with the risk of getting a hole in their stockings, stockings that were knitted (there was no nylon at that time), I don't know how stockings are made nowadays but at that time ... the hole would suddenly make a ladder down the stocking and I can still see the gesture, a bit familiar, a bit trivial, but necessary, whereby a woman would wet a finger in her mouth and apply it to the weave, cementing it with saliva, and in this way she would stop it (what's more, I remember there used to be, close by to our apartment on the rue de Seine, near the rue Jacques-Calot, a very tiny stall of *stoppeuses*, that is, of workers whose working lives were spent 'stopping' stockings and sometimes other items of clothing).

189

This is what writing is, says Barthes. I would say: this is what writing is. This is what the actual setting down of writing as distinct from the fantasy of writing is: a kind of catch or halt or temporary immobilization in the run of culture.

Likewise, to my mind, if I can venture this: the translator wets her finger, she presses it down on the run of alternatives, the run of endless translation possibilities, each one with its own particular shades of meaning. And right now, in this moment, if only for her moment, familiarly and necessarily, and with all the delicate immobilizing power of saliva on wool, she makes it stop.

Still in the library, in the small arena of translation, I remember sitting for a long time with the found poem, the book hinged between summer and autumn, looking around at all the quiet readers (finger still in my mouth), not yet quite ready to make up my mind.

AMATEUR TRANSLATOR

The Saturday morning exerciser likes dancing a lot. She goes every week. She doesn't exactly have an end in sight – a goal, that is. No one comes to watch her (she would probably hate it if they did). She appreciates the scale of the class: it is too large for anything like individual attention; the instructor doesn't correct or evaluate her. She is getting marginally better at following the steps, possibly, because she goes every week. But the point has never been to impress, to instruct or to entertain anyone else. She's clearly not a professional; her aim is not to professionalize her activity. Not only because she's not especially good at it but because to do so would bring the expectations of others, like a weight. She is practising for no obvious purpose other than the repeated pleasure of it (*'amator*: one who loves and loves again,' writes Barthes in Richard Howard's translation). Insofar as she is content to practise indefinitely, she is very unlike the writer, the artist video-maker or indeed the translator, who might one day publish her translation, attach her name to it and help publicize the new commodity she has played her part in making (which, in this time of boom, is a bit more likely to be asked of her). And yet, what connects this space of exercise to the practice of translation – in my own head, at least – is something like the open invitation of it. The idea that, in principle, and unlike the more exclusive dance classes I have tried out and suffered in before: here, anyone can come along and join in.

This is of the order of a fantasy, clearly. There may well be a range of bodies in the gym above the swimming pool – mostly women, a wide-ish range of the ages, shapes, ethnicities commensurate with the diversity of Paris's thirteenth arrondissement. But the range is limited: by no means all bodies and experiences are represented. It's a fantasy: an image of shared and open access to an energetic practice – bodies working out, repeating, in our individual ways, the moves that we receive delightedly from someone else – that I offer for translation. It's a fantasy, I know: my own beautiful heterotopia. But I set it down here nonetheless.

I am a translator and a writer, or so I claim, when asked what I do, professionally speaking. As a way of making the writing part clear – in case it were not already obvious. In recognition of the fact that it is very often not already obvious. When I teach translation (I am a translator and a writer and a tutor), I am often surprised by how often students are surprised to discover that translating involves writing, that its most vital prerequisite is an interest in writing, for the reason that written translations have to be written. Where the *would-be* of it is wholly appropriate because *how to do this* and indeed *whether or not I am capable of doing this* are questions whose answers are in no way given in advance. 'Hundreds of times I have sat, for hours on end, before passages whose meaning I understood perfectly, without seeing how to render them into English,' wrote Arthur Waley, 'a genius of translation', whose line is quoted by Simon Leys in an essay on literary translation translated by Dan Gunn. In other words, it is possible to be a highly experienced and acclaimed translator and yet still be altogether incapable of predicting the kinds of writing questions (the troubles and challenges) that a given sentence will present. Or to know from the outset how to resolve them. But then I remember that I too once thought of translation as essentially a test of linguistic and cultural competence: a live audit undertaken for the purposes of establishing what I knew – what I should, by then, have already known – about the French language and culture. This was how it was presented to me, to a line of us hating our translation class on our year abroad: as an on-the-spot diagnostic, an occasion to show up, with reference to a pre-prepared model-answer, how much we were getting wrong.

A little art, is how Helen Lowe-Porter described it in the 1950s. A little art, as distinct from the big ones. Neither very important nor very serious. But limited, modest. Something young (as if translating were not as old as speaking itself) and therefore easy to patronize. We could argue at length about how unhelpful this characterization is, and how retrograde. You could point out all the ways and I would listen and I would agree. I would wholeheartedly agree. One way of countering the still widespread undervaluing of the work of translation might be to stress the extent of the translator's skill and expertise. I thought of this recently, reading an essay titled 'Translation as Scholarship' by Catherine Porter. An academic, translator and President of the Modern Languages Association, Porter makes a powerful case for 'scholarly and literary translations' being 'accepted and evaluated on the same basis as scholarly monographs in decisions about hiring, promotion and tenure' in an academic career. The 'skilled translator-scholar' described in Porter's essay is – crucially – already skilled (and already a translator and already a scholar) before she begins: this is what helps her to determine what is 'deemed worthy of translation' in the first place, before bringing her 'prior knowledge of the field, and thoroughgoing mastery of at least two languages and cultures, plus highly developed research skills and a healthy measure of critical acumen' to bear on the process itself. Porter concludes her essay thus: 'Unless we believe that the only literature worth reading and the only scholarship of value are produced in English and perhaps in the handful of other languages that we happen to know, we need to acknowledge that reliable translations produced by accomplished scholar-translators are crucial to the continuing development of our fields. Once we have done that, we should be ready to rewrite our personnel policies so as to recognize these scholar-translators as full-fledged colleagues and evaluate their work accordingly.'

I read the same kinds of arguments being made for literary translation, too. In an article dealing in part with the responses to Janet Malcolm's controversial *New York Review of Books* essay 'Socks', in which she writes in praise of Constance Garnett's Tolstoy translations (and is deeply critical of Richard Pevear and Larissa Volokhonsky's retranslations), the scholar Caryl Emerson quotes a letter to the *NYRB* from Judson Rosengrant, 'a professional translator of Tolstoy'. Rosengrant had offered a detailed case study of a single word as it appears in *Anna Karenina* – a verb favoured by Stivia Oblonsky (*obrazuetsia* – 'it will come right'). Reading Rosengrant's 'tour de force' account of the morphology and semantics of the verb 'reminded me,' writes Emerson, 'of how much we need to know, especially with a fastidious craftsman like Tolstoy, in order to translate the simplest utterance appropriate to the psychology of the fictive person who utters it'.

How much we need to know,
in order to.

'It is a pleasure,' writes Dorothy Bussy to Gide in a letter from November 1931, 'to have even the smallest thing to do for you.' (Gide had asked for her assessment of a draft translation he'd received of his *Corydon*.) But the fact is, this translation is terrible: it is 'utterly, hopelessly, impossibly bad'. She lists the ways:

'The translator doesn't know the rudiments of either French or English.

He doesn't understand the commonest French idioms: *on a beau, tout au plus, il y a de quoi, faire le jeu de, faire grâce de, savoir gré à qq., tenir à qq., etc. etc.*

He confuses: *se tuer* and *se taire, atteindre à* and *attendre, jouir* and *jouer, réseau* and *réserve, rétaquer* and *réfuter* with disastrous results to the sense.

Translates *factice* several times over by facetious.

He fails utterly to follow the argument and constantly puts the vital clause in the negative when it ought to be in the affirmative and vice versa.

He has no idea of the value and very little of the meaning of particles and conjunctions such as *en effet, pourtant, enfin*, etc. etc.

Dozens of his sentences mean either the contrary of the French, or have no meaning at all, or are incomprehensible unless compared with the original.

His English is no better.

His use of auxiliaries is the strangest I have ever seen.

Will, shall, can, may used as in no English or American I have ever met.

His prepositions are fantastic.

As for elegance, subtlety, distinction, Heavens!'

A little later on in the letter she writes: '[I]t is incomprehensible to me why a man who understands a book so little should want to translate it or how a man who knows so little of a language should think he is capable of translating it. Mysteries!'

First, there is established and wide-ranging linguistic and cultural competence, so the argument goes. There is bilingualism, or what is sometimes called 'near-native-competence', and in-depth knowledge of both cultures. There must also be, for Porter, reading and writing and research skills, plus critical acumen. *Then*, and *only then*, can there be something like translation. If, that is, we want to avoid the kind of translation-disaster, the failure that Bussy describes (the quality of any eventual translation attesting to – offering a kind of diagnostic of – the degree to which this knowledge foundation was already in place). I can see the logic and necessity of these arguments. But still I am wondering: is this always how things are? How they should be?

I recently met a very lovely woman at a wedding. She was telling me about a family holiday to Normandy – idle days. How in the house they were renting for the week there was a copy of the first Harry Potter novel in French translation, the book that her daughter happened to be reading in the original at the time. Just out of curiosity, and with very little French, she found herself having a go at translating the translation. To see if she could make her way back to the original English, but finding herself very often quite far to one side of it. And it was interesting, she said. In fact, it was totally fascinating – her face alight with it. The casual exercise ended up preoccupying all the quiet moments of her holiday. But of course it really doesn't count, though, does it? is how she concluded her story, the light leaving her face. I mean, what I was doing – it wasn't *really* translating was it? Not in the way you do it or understand it.

Here is an example of a different form of collective exercise: a Dutch-to-English literary translation group which convenes very irregularly in Rotterdam. Five of us with an interest in reading and writing and a desire to learn more about Dutch literature. One native Dutch-speaker, the rest of us with different kinds of English and beginners' level Dutch. We work in Leeszaal, sometimes, the community space on Rijnhoutplein, or in the public library or under the trees in the park. We began with the project of translating some of A. L. Snijders's very short animal stories for the reason that they are very short and so offered us the chance of translating a whole. And for the further reason that Lydia Davis had recently published some of her own translations of these stories in the online journal *Asymptote*, versions against which we would eventually compare our own. Real-life examples that are problematic in the same ways: the woman at the wedding working on Harry Potter; our group translating short stories that have already been touched and translated – and so in this sense validated – by a celebrated English-language translator. Our choices of what to amateurishly translate have so far been predictable and repetitive. But we are all beginning. In Rotterdam we have moved on, now, to as yet unpublished work that the Dutch speaker finds of interest and scans for us. We work very slowly: translating a sentence can take up all the afternoon.

My feeling is – this experience tells me – that translation *can* get started. That translation can start. Not from established competence or experience, always and necessarily, but with, let's say: a piece of writing written in another language, a dictionary, an online translation tool, a forum where you can post questions, or friends who speak the language whom you can talk to and argue with. I have discovered and tested this – in the translation workshops that I have initiated and taken part in, where we all undertake to translate a piece of writing written in a language no one in the room can speak. As an exercise, an experiment, to see just how close to or how far away we can get from the existing published translations that we may or may not eventually allow into the room. I am perpetually rediscovering and retesting this in the context of our Dutch-to-English translation group. I believe – the very idea of our working group is premised on the shared belief – that it is possible for us to find out what the sentences in the Dutch stories mean. To establish more or less and to be overwhelmed and perplexed by the range of their likely meanings. On the condition, that is, that we spend enough time with them: the length of the time and with the quality of attention that the project of translating demands of us. Which might be fast – there is no reason why translation can't get done a bit faster –, but in our case happens to be very, very slow.

The idea of the unschooled (or to borrow Jacques Rancière's term, the 'ignorant') translator, translating work written in a language she makes no real claim to know, by a writer whose culture she has no real lived or extended close experience of, is a difficult one. It is very fraught, this question of who can be trusted with the work of representing the speech, the writing, the work of someone else: who is learned enough, who is experienced enough, who is sensitive and careful enough. The question becomes more difficult still when we consider the uneven dynamics of any translation relation, and especially the English-language translator's real power. I would be unconvinced by any account of the work of translation that ignores this. Because it's true: undertaking a translation, I may well learn nothing. I may end up making work that unknowingly does violence to the original writing: misunderstanding it, forcing it to adapt and conform to my own desire for it, my fantasy of what it represents for me, closing it down rather than opening myself and others up to it. Getting led nowhere by the exercise of translation other than back into what I already presumed to know about the writing (the language, the culture) in question. But, at the same time, I would be unconvinced by an account of translating that passes too quickly over or fails altogether to notice its *chance* of learning. The chance it offers of becoming- expert, becoming-linguistically and culturally competent, becoming-critical, becoming-intimate, becoming a better – or, if not a better (because are we really getting any better at reading and writing? Is it useful to think of these activities in terms of progress?) – then certainly a *different* reader and writer. Translation as the chance – a translation project as a means of giving oneself the chance – of being taught by the other's writing, where answers to the questions of *how* to be responsible for this writing, and *whether or not you or I will be capable* of taking responsibility for this writing are, again, in no way given in advance.

Too quickly and too fast. So fast, in fact, that the thing disappears, as if down a trapdoor. When I read translation described in terms of 'thorough-going mastery', personally, I can no longer recognize it.

To be clear: it is not my intention to downplay the knowledge that is involved in translating (Oh yeah, it sounds hard but actually, as it turns out, anyone can do it: really, just look at the woman on her lovely holiday; just look at us translating for fun and leisurely from the Dutch). Nor is it to absolve anyone of the requirement to learn new languages. (Gayatri Spivak is brilliant on this: 'If you are interested in talking about the other,' she writes, 'and/or in making a claim to be the other, it is crucial to learn other languages.') It's rather to offer a view of translation as a *site* for learning through reading and writing, through testing and researching, through asking and arguing, in the hope of extending the invitation to do translations to more of us (why not to all of us?).

Because (to put the same point another way): at what prior stage in her education would – or could – the translator presume to *already* know enough? To have *already* read widely and closely enough? To be fully linguistically and culturally competent enough? Tell me, really: when could anyone, any reader or writer, consider themselves adequately *pre*-qualified to undertake the translation of, say, a 730-page novel set in a sanatorium? One of Germany's most formative contributions to European literature? Or indeed an unpublished story by a Dutch artist – his first effort at fiction? It seems to me that translators undertake to write translations not as a means to demonstrate their expertise but precisely because they know, without yet knowing exactly how or in what particular ways, doing so will be productive of *new* knowledge. As yet un-acquired, un-grounded knowledge of the world – of experiences and stories, ideas and things, people and places, tastes and smells, rhythms and sounds. Knowledge of the world as well as, always, and always in the form of, *writing*. Passing over this in the name of promoting the status of translation and translators risks passing over what I consider to be the most powerful argument for its interest. While at the same time making exclusive what might otherwise be its more open and shared adventure. Do translations! Yes, yes and absolutely. But who are we saying can?

When the gym is so full of bodies I can't see the instructor, I copy the woman in front of me, and the woman behind me copies me in turn. In this way we share the moves around. We get to dance them – the pleasure of actually getting to dance them! Someone else's moves, only this time made with my own body – falling in and out of sync with each other, with the music, with hip hop, tango, ballet.

Among the distributed topics that make up Barthes's autobiography, translated by Richard Howard as *Roland Barthes by Roland Barthes,* there is one titled '*La jeune fille bourgeoise*', a title translated by Howard as 'The middle-class maiden'. It comes immediately before the paragraph in praise of the 'Amateur', and in many ways prefigures it.

'Middle-class maiden' – I actually like how wrong and untimely that sounds (a synonym for lady translator?).

The paragraph she titles begins: 'Surrounded by political upheaval, he plays the piano, paints watercolours.'

Who does?

The pronoun switch is for a moment confusing.

Before it becomes clear that Barthes does.

It is Barthes who occupies – who, here, is claiming for himself – the position of the middle-class maiden: playing the piano and painting watercolours in his apartment in Paris's sixth arrondissement. He's the one who would regularly engage in what he calls all the false – or fake? sham? (*les faux*) – occupations of another era's accomplished young lady. How to justify such leisured activities? 'Surrounded by political upheaval...' how to justify the piano-playing, the watercolour-painting, the Saturday morning exercise, the amateur translating?

There he is: this is the scene that Barthes offers us. Barthes as the middle-class maiden, producing uselessly, stupidly (*bêtement,* writes Barthes – mindlessly?), and seemingly only for his/her own pleasure, for his/her own distraction and instruction.

But be that as it may, the point for Barthes is that still she *produced*. Still, he writes, 'she was producing'. Of the middle-class young maiden's unprofessionalized and yet still productive activity, he affirms: *C'était sa forme de dépense à elle.*

A sentence translated by Howard as: 'It was her own form of expenditure.'

Is there a way of ending, appositionally, on the *elle*, I wonder? Reproducing the emphasis of the *à elle*?

Awkwardly: it was her form of using energy proper to her.

Or, it was her way of expending energy – for her.

What Barthes finds of interest in the activities of the middle-class maiden is not her repetition, her re-inscription of some erstwhile aspect of bourgeois life. It is instead, as Adrien Chassain argues in a detailed discussion of Barthes's investment in the amateur, how she seems to be exceeding her role in it. It is something like the affirmation that he sees in her ongoing commitment to such privileged activities: this private assertion of her own energy and potentiality. An energy that she expends without any ambition of ever producing a finished worldly product – but that is still productive nevertheless.

Of what though?

What – to use Barthes's term – might be the utopia of such apparently unproductive productive activities?

I find an answer – at least, I think I find the suggestion of an answer – in a lesson plan for children that Barthes once offered in an interview.

Titled 'Literature / Teaching' and published in 1975, the interview pertains to the teaching of literature in schools. Can 'literature' be taught? was among the questions asked. And, if so, how? Barthes's answer, translated by Linda Coverdale, unfolds in stages:

'People are usually concerned with content in the teaching of language and literature,' he says. 'But the task involves much more than that. It also involves the relations between and the shared presence of living bodies. The real problem is to learn how a class in language or literature can be filled with values or desires that are not accommodated by the institution, when they're not being actively repressed by it.'

'It seems to me,' he goes on, 'that if I were facing a classroom of students, my chief concern would be to find out what is desired. It would not be a question of wanting to liberate desires, nor even of learning what they might be (which would be an enormous undertaking in any case), but of asking the question: "Is there desire?"'

In seminars, the smaller and more intimate pedagogical settings of the EHESS (where Barthes was teaching prior to his appointment at the Collège de France), 'there is always desire,' he recounts. The students attend because of their own desires, using the thesis (the writing of a doctoral thesis) as a pretext for writing. He says: 'There is always, deep inside, a desire for writing. People come because I have written.' This of course is not likely to be the case in the school classroom. How then to enable the possibility of reading and writing pleasure there? How to open up reading and writing as practices so that the schoolchildren might share in them, too?

Well, why not try something like this: give children 'the opportunity to create whole objects, over a long period of time'. As such, the exercise would be something quite different from the usual homework assignment. Imagine each pupil being asked to create a whole work, and setting him or herself all the tasks necessary to its completion. Why not offer children a real possibility of structuring the object to be created? Without, he adds, 'reifying any eventual outcome', but engaging instead with what, in the light of the lecture course he delivered three years later, we might call its 'preparation'. (The lesson plan reads like an outline for the project of *The Preparation of the Novel*.) This, Barthes suggests, would do two things. First, it would open children up to the pleasures of producing for its own sake, before it reaches the circuits of esteem, grades or commercialization. Second, it would offer a different point of entry into literature, a way of sharing in the making of it. It would give them access to literature as a storehouse of possible forms to be copied, relayed and circulated amongst themselves.

At stake in all this is how the works that get distributed by professionals in the public sphere come to meet and interact with the daily lives of those who do not occupy that sphere, or not in the same way, and not with the same agency: children, for example; or the bored privileged young woman at her piano, her synthesizer, her iPhone. How these forms might be made to circulate more widely in the social field, while also recognizing the manners in which they are already circulating, the ways in which they are already being extended and modified, corrupted and re-energized by the less visible agents of that circulation, where the field also includes the classroom, the gym above the swimming pool, the bourgeois living room. The middle-class maiden's productivity, practising in her own private amateur mode, is of value because she represents – she both enacts and represents – one of the ways in which things get made to move, how forms travel, how they get tried out, passing from body to body, from the public sphere into the private and back again. Reading Chassain's discussion, I am struck by a line he quotes from a very early review Barthes wrote of a chamber music concert: 'A society is beautiful only to the extent that there's a natural circulation between the works of its great men and the intimate life of its individuals and its homes.'

Creative writing exercises for everyone!

Aerobics classes with a mishmash of dance moves for everyone!

Translation for everyone!

Is that right?

Yes and why not?

This is the fantasy. It is the order of a fantasy, I know: where aerobics meets translation at the level of energy and instruction and pleasure, a means to try out and learn from, to share in and repurpose the gestures and moves we receive from elsewhere. From the works of 'great men' and women (the theorist and scholar Marielle Macé has recently made a brilliant case for the way our reading informs our living in precisely these terms, and her thinking informs my own here). As well as, vitally and hopefully, from the incalculable number of as yet unread and as yet unrecognized works whose new reception, here, in our individual lives and homes, might be the chance of expanding and nuancing, of querying the terms of the category we receive as 'great'. A fantasy where the invitation of translation is opened out to more of us, with the assurance – the sense of new permission – that comes with the claim that translation can start, that it need only take, at the outset, something like desire, or curiosity, or some prior or suggested interest in a bit of writing written in another language, in the work of someone else written somewhere else. Bringing no guarantee that the translations produced will be any good, necessarily – that they will reach the standards of the professionals. But perhaps that doesn't always have to be the point. An invitation to translate that would in turn depend on a willingness to embrace (rather than worry over) the constitutive amateurishness of the translator. The way translation starts – always to some degree, I think, regardless of previous experience – from a position of not knowing. Not knowing what the task, this time, will entail, not knowing whether, this time, I will be capable of it, not knowing what the doing of it – the fact of me doing it, right here and now – will make happen. But the way it creates a scene – a domestic scene, a classroom scene, a bourgeois living-room scene or a mum-on-holiday-with-her-kids scene – for learning (for testing and finding out) nonetheless. A little bit of translating, a little bit of engagement with the world in the mode offered by this very particular art. The *little* set down here with no intention of downplaying anything at all, but as a way of taking measure of the ways energies get expended of a regular weekly morning, of an occasional afternoon, or every single day over a lifetime. Think of the committed Saturday morning exerciser, the way she takes the moves she learns in the gym home, whacking them out, now, on the living room floor. How she essays them – how she might at this very moment be re-essaying them and sharing them, putting them into new circulation as she dances dodgily with her family and friends. I offer amateur translation as a means to do the same, only this time with sentences, only this time with the kick and different beat of a sentence written in another language: *C'était sa forme de dépense à elle.*

Yes, but (Bussy asked): 'Why would someone who understands a book so little ... want to translate it? Why should someone who knows so little of a language ... think he [or she] is capable of translating it?' I've not forgotten her bafflement at the bad translation, her dismay at the presumptuousness of the unnamed translator. Nor indeed Timothy Buck's inventory of Helen Lowe-Porter's translation mistakes.

I think again of Barthes's imagined lesson plan, the way it seems to prefigure, so unexpectedly, the project of the last lecture course. Not a little bit of writing now and then, to be picked up and dropped again, casually, when the mood takes him. That doesn't describe the intensive and durational writing project he set himself late in life, in the form of a two-year series of public lectures. The point was rather to 'create' – (to have the opportunity of creating) – 'whole objects, over a long period of time'. Whole objects like a whole work of literature. Like, for example, the entirety of a very short short-story. Like, in Barthes's case, a novel. Like a lecture course on the preparation of a novel. Or indeed its translation. The translator as a maker of wholes. Where the requirement of the whole, the requirement that the translator attend to the whole, serves not as a safeguard against 'utterly, hopelessly, impossibly bad' translation. But more as an indication of the work still to come.

MAKER OF WHOLES
(LET'S SAY OF A TABLE)

The first time I visited the Bibliothèque François Mitterand, with its tall glass corner towers, I had no idea about the sunken forest garden. Approaching the library from a distance I remember mistaking the trees for shrubs, which I assumed to be knee- or even ankle-height. It was this slow giddy tilt when I realized that in fact they were the crowns of trees, sprung from branches and then from trunks, and how deeply they plunged. It turns out that the tallest are sycamore pines. On the library's website you can read about how, as part of the construction of the new site in the mid-1990s, hundreds of trees – birches, oaks and hornbeams, as well as the 165 sycamore pines – were uprooted from a real forest two hundred kilometres away, to be transported and replanted here, making a replica forest garden. And, it so happens, a passing home for starlings. Pasted every now and then along the inner windows of the research rooms are these big blue stickers: graphic shapes of bigger birds silhouetted from above or below. I think the idea is to startle the starlings, and make them indirectly aware of the glass.

Looking sideways onto that transplanted portion of forest, at a desk in one of the lower-level reading rooms, I'm told there is a researcher currently working on *Bouvard and Pécuchet*, Gustave Flaubert's last, unfinished novel.

As part of his novel-writing project, Flaubert is said to have read a great many books. The final estimate is something extraordinary. In the introduction to his recent retranslation of the novel, Mark Polizzotti puts it at some fifteen hundred.

And the researcher, well.

The story I heard about the researcher is that she is reading them again. That is, *every single one of the books* that Flaubert read in order to have his characters read them, or bits of them, as they try and mostly fail, comically, to apply their learning to life.

In the same sequence? I don't know.

I hope so.

I can't tell you any more about the researcher because I've never spoken to her. I don't know her name. I've never even had her pointed out to me. I have no idea how she thinks about her project: this dedicated retracing of someone else's reading path, cut through the stacks of some other reading room well over a century previously. Whether she is close to finishing, or – perhaps? – has given up altogether. But the giddy tilt I felt upon discovering that the shrubs planted in the heart of the library were actually trees – it was the same delighted unnerving feeling when I first heard the story about her work.

I'll read the books that Barthes read, I told myself, when starting out on the project of translating his lectures. Ideally, in the order in which he read them. This would be my own directed reading programme. For what purpose, exactly? To find the passages in the works he quotes, of course; also, to be in a better position to follow the arguments he makes. Yes, but what else? To know something, a part of what he knew? To experience some thing – even to feel something – that he felt and he experienced? The desire for a novel, for example, so wholly bound up with his reading of Tolstoy, and especially, essentially, of Proust? It sounds a bit unlikely now.

Reading the same books as someone else is a way of being together. This is the premise of seminars, book-clubs, of so many friendships and conversations. What it is to discover that you're currently reading the same book as someone else – especially someone you don't know all that well. The startling, sometimes discomforting, effect of accelerated intimacy, as if that person had gone from standing across the room to all of a sudden holding your hand.

But then again, what kind of shared experience is this? Who's to say that when reading *The Life and Adventures of Robinson Crusoe*, for example, a novel which occupies a privileged place in the first lecture course, I'll notice what Barthes noticed, think what Barthes thought, experience what he experienced? Or even: that I'll pause where he paused, looking up from the page where he did? The novel is of interest to Barthes because of its status as a novel of solitude, or living-alone. In *How to Live Together*, it offers a way into thinking about what might be community's opposite term. A lecture course whose founding fantasy, he tells us, developed out of the chance encounter with a word. It was while reading an academic article on the monasteries of Mount Athos, says Barthes, that I happened across this beautiful new word: 'idiorrhythmy'. A chance encounter, a chance reading: Barthes's phrase is *une lecture gratuite*, an adjective I turned over and over in the effort to translate it. Not a gratuitous reading or a purposeless reading exactly. But something more like an as-yet-un-instrumentalized reading: reading for its own sake; reading with no expectation of being made useful or for the purposes of anything else. It was in the course of such a reading, says Barthes, that I came across the word that would open out a whole new direction of inquiry: the forms of community that might accommodate the particular life-rhythms of each individual ('idiorrhythmy' is made from idios + rhythm). Barthes's deliberately unsystematic method is to go where the word leads him: to be led, to be pulled by this word, and to attend to those various tugging forces: to allow himself to stumble, as he puts it, among snatches, fragments, between tastes and flavours, the bounds of different fields of knowledge (again, the proximity he points up, in French, between the words *saveur* and *savoir*). An unorthodox mode of proceeding, perhaps, for a lecture course delivered in the academic setting of the Collège de France. But is this not how reading generally happens? The point seems to be this: left to its own devices, the path of reading is very rarely chronologically ordered, thematically coherent, limited by language or respectful of borders. Books open out onto, they cross with and follow haphazardly on from one another. Left to its own devices, the path of reading strays all over the place.

And then along comes the translator, thinking of the re-searcher in the library, determined to walk that straying path all over again.

There can be many different motivations for doing or making something again, only this time in your own setting and doing it yourself. It might be that you need your own version of it, or others do. It might be a way of bringing the extant thing closer, or for you to draw closer to it. It can be a way of understanding what the extant thing is or was, and a way of making it behave or mean differently – producing new knowledge and understanding. It can also be a form of entertainment. A friend tells me about a film called *Living with the Tudors* by artists Karen Guthrie and Nina Pope, which narrates their time spent living among a community of historical re-enactors. She describes a distinction that Guthrie and Pope posit in relation to their work. Which is the difference between doing something again in the name of newness and doing something new in the name of againness. I'm delighted by this: giddy again, and unnerved. And after some deliberation I think I would place translation in the second category. Here is a translation. Here is a thing often (if not always) conscious of and keen to gesture toward its origins, to its already existing first manifestation. This is the frame of againness, the name in which you are invited to receive it (and indeed compelled, by copyright law, to receive it). Even as the materials and the manner, the agent and the occasion of making, as well as the thing itself, are all new.

Look to the whole, Helen Lowe-Porter asked (of the readers of her translations).

But what kind of maker and of what kind of whole is the translator with her translation?

Let's say – I want to propose now, as a device to think awhile with – a table-maker. The maker of a table.

But with a very specific scene of making in mind: Robinson Crusoe on his undeserted island, making a table again in what for him will be the first time.

Robinson Crusoe – what 'a dismal book', declares George Orwell in an essay from 1949 on Charles Reade, the nineteenth-century novelist, whose *Foul Play* is for Orwell an altogether superior example of the desert-island novel. Unlike Defoe, Reade was 'an expert on desert islands,' writes Orwell. 'Or at any rate he was very well up in the geography textbooks of the time. *Robinson Crusoe*,' on the other hand, is a book 'so unreadable as a whole that few people even know that the second part exists.'

For Barthes, too, by far the best bit is the long first part: all the small differences it makes between the days. Here is Robinson Crusoe alone on and anxiously claiming his island. Here he is planting things, sometimes writing. Here he is recording the weather. It is, Barthes remarks, an oddly *event-less* novel; its charm lies in its low-key unfolding.

Yes, it's truly 'a dismal book', wrote Orwell. That said, no desert-island story 'is altogether bad when it sticks to the actual concrete details of the struggle to keep alive'. In this regard, even Defoe's novel 'becomes interesting when it describes Crusoe's efforts to make a table'. From my Wordsworth Classics edition of *Robinson Crusoe*:

'And now I began to apply myself to make such necessary things as I found I wanted, particularly a chair and a table; for without these I was not able to enjoy the few comforts I had in the world; I could not write or eat, or do several things, with so much pleasure without a table. So I went to work.

And here I must needs observe that as reason is the substance and origin of the mathematics, so by stating and squaring everything by reason, and by making the most rational judgement of things, every man may in time be the master of every mechanic art. I had never handled a tool in my life, and yet in time, by labour, application, and contrivance, I found at last that I wanted nothing but I could have made it, especially if I had had tools; however, I made abundance of things even without tools, and some with no more tools than an adze and a hatchet, which were perhaps never made that way before, and that with infinite labour. For example, if I wanted a board, I had no other way but to cut down a tree, set it on an edge before me, and hew it flat on either side with my axe, till I had brought it to be as thin as a plank, and then dub it smooth with my adze. It is true, by this method I could make but one board out of a whole tree, but this I had no remedy for but patience, any more than I had for the prodigious deal of time and labour which it took me up to make a plank or board. But my time or labour was little worth, and so it was as well employed one way as another.'

To be clear: in this account, it takes one whole tree to make but one solitary board.

Then, eventually, in the long run of it, enough whole trees are fashioned into a table.

So this is *infinite* labour.

Immeasurable, boundless labour.

Labour that's invested in reason but on the side of the unthinkable, the impossible.

Labour that's invested in making the most rational judgement of things but on the side of the excessive, the irrational.

Labour that's framed as necessity, undertaken in response to a pressing demand. But when the demands are so diverse and so many – Why a table right now and not a boat? – it springs (it must spring?), also, from desire and out of curiosity.

Labour that seems to aspire, at the outset, only to repetition. But turns out to require *contrivance*. That is to say, new skill, improvisation and different invention.

Labour that's for the moment undivided (he will make the whole table himself).

Labour that's quite comically laborious.

But then again, as Robinson Crusoe points out: Why not? It's not as if there's any urgency. Or, to put it another way, cast alone upon a desolate island, who's to say what urgent means? Presumably, the matter of how fast things need to get done, what counts as quick here and what counts as slow, can be decided again.

When people discuss the economic realities of literary translation, they often point out how difficult it is – to the point of impossible, as my professor warned me – to make a living from it. Boyd Tonkin, the founder of the Independent Foreign Fiction Prize, makes the point in a recent article titled 'Labours of Love'. Despite the increasing interest in literature in translation (the boom sounded by Rachel Cooke in the *Observer*) 'the translation of literature,' he writes, 'will seldom seem like a sane choice of career. Although rates and contracts vary enormously, the UK Translators' Association currently advises that "we have found that UK publishers are prepared to pay in the region of £90 per 1,000 words." Labours of love, indeed.' Insane, then, because the work involved in writing a translation seems to be so clearly in excess of – so out of proportion and unbalanced in relation to – its small material returns.

'And now I began to apply myself to such necessary things as I found I wanted.'

Is the table, for Robinson Crusoe, a necessary thing?

Yes, of course. Yes, on the one hand. Yes, in the sense that everything he makes on his island will be useful. Robinson Crusoe, the careful recorder of his time and investment, balancing in his journal his input and output, produces only for use, not for exchange. Although it is true that there's no one (or not yet anyone) around to exchange with.

Robinson Crusoe needs a table.

But the further point seems to be: he would like a table. A table is among the necessary things 'he found he wanted'. He wanted a table because it was wanting. Or, the table was wanting because he wanted it. For the enabling comforts of a surface to write on, to eat off. But also: the table as the marker, the proxemical centre of the European home, of what will become Robinson Crusoe's castle, standing in for the power he'll come to wield over his re-made civilization. A proxemical object like the fireplace or a lamp or the TV – the kinds of objects that Barthes discusses in a session of *How to Live Together*: objects that we tend to gather around, in proximity, configuring our bodies, our spaces and our other objects in relation to them. In his lectures, Barthes notes how Robinson Crusoe seems to have no problem making rectangles (the chair, the table, the walls of his fortress), but a good deal of trouble with circles (the wheel in the wheelbarrow, the barrel). 'The rectangle [is] the basic shape of power,' he writes. And the table is desired, ultimately, for its powerful symbolic value. But in the meantime there's also the invested occupation that making it provides. A further motor of the project is curiosity: the fantasy of a table set down as a problem to be solved. What would it entail for

Robinson Crusoe to make a table here and now, in these new, rough and rude circumstances? Will he – with his limited skills, his different materials, his faith in reason – be up to the task of finding out? For the instruction of it? For the life-structuring *project* of it? Elsewhere in the lectures Barthes describes the project – in French the *projet* – as a kind of projectile, something a person throws out ahead of themselves, as one way among others of organizing the days.

Given the way the translator's per-word fee refuses to tally with the time and effort involved, and given how hard it is (how hard I find it) to speed up – to translate faster in order to make this per-word fee work in the translator's favour – perhaps somewhere in the mix of her motivations there's the different promise of cultural capital. Tonkin's article, with its investment in the translator's selflessness, her generosity, her altruism, her uncomplicated love, makes no room for this at all. But perhaps the translator *is* betting on the possibility, somewhere out there on the horizon, that she might one day exchange the fact of having translated this writer's work into English, a writer whose already established prestige and recognition – or as yet untapped potential for prestige and recognition – she is drawing on (or indeed, positioning herself as being the very first person to point to: 'Spotlight your favourite underrepresented languages!' ran the tagline for a recent competition for emerging translators). Exchange it for a new translation commission, or a teaching post, or a publication contract to write an essay on the practice of translation. Indeed, if I am now gainfully employed (as a part-time tutor in a university and an art school), perhaps it *is* in large part down to having done this; down to the five or so years it took to translate the two volumes of lecture notes having its own currency, a currency that I was eventually in a position to exchange for a job.

I think again of the researcher in the library, sitting at her desk-island, undertaking her monumental and discreet undertaking. Reading her way through Flaubert's enormous list of books at her own, presumably different pace, unwitnessed by the other concentrated bodies, the birds and the trees.

There's every chance, I realize, that she's planning to one day convert her labour into pieces of scholarship: a sequence of articles, or a monograph, say, that in themselves are very unlikely to bring her any financial reward. Work that will perhaps come to be valued for the contribution it makes to knowledge, to Flaubert scholarship, that might come in time to boost her credibility, her standing, her chances of promotion. There's every chance that she, too, is speculating. But what kind of long-term speculation is this? I remember reading an interview with the novelist and critic Adam Thirlwell, who had just published a book telling the many adventures of the novel in translation. When asked if he'd consider doing a full-length translation himself (in addition to the French-English translation of the Vladimir Nabokov story that is included as an appendix to *The Delighted States*), his answer was to say: 'I'd love there to be more translated from South American writers from the early twentieth century: Roberto Arlt, Macedonio Fernández. Then a more complete version of Central Europeans like Bohumil Hrabal. And also more from less well-known periods of major literatures, like the libertine French novels of the eighteenth century, by novelists like Crébillon fils. As for me, though, I don't know when I'll ever undertake any of these. I was asked by my publisher if I wanted to translate *Madame Bovary* – which initially excited me and then I thought of the time it would take – about the time, basically, it would take to write *Madame Bovary*. I wish more novelists translated novels, but novelists, rightly, in a way, are selfish, and translation of long works takes up so much time.'

The translation of long works takes up so much time.

In the meantime, one could have written a novel: my own monographic thing.

What's more, even when they do get finally finished: 'Glory, for the translator, is borrowed glory.' Or so Tim Parks recently announced in a column for the *New York Review of Books*. And 'there's no way round this'. Parks's point is that a translator's work is celebrated if and only if the work she is translating is worth celebrating; there is no separating her achievement from that of its original author. As a consequence of this, Parks argues, mediocre translators of successful books sometimes get unduly praised, while those more talented translators translating less visible works hardly get noticed at all.

I think part of what Parks says is true: the translator's achievement is indeed inseparable from that of the original author. I also think that the translator, altogether conscious of the collaborative, intensely relational nature of her work – of the fact that she is always translating *something* by *someone else* – is unlikely ever to dispute the inseparability of her achievement. For me, what this suggests is that accompanying (or undermining) the translator's calculation, her opportunism, her quest for borrowed glory – if indeed, there has been such speculation; if, indeed, she has been conscious of it – there is something always a bit untallyable about her project. Translating takes such a long time, it's true, which means that its promise of cultural capital is only ever a distant promise. What's more, if and when it does come her way, according to Parks it would appear to have no *authentic* or especially *stable* value anyway. Or at least no value that can't very easily be disputed and taken away ('borrowed glory' – Parks's phrase is deeply and strikingly suspicious). In these terms, writing translations doesn't make a great deal of sense; it's altogether illogical according to the logics that we are all supposed to be contained and explained by (the ongoing and ever more efficient accumulation of status, money and things). Which suggests to me that there's something resistant in this: about undertaking a project – a great life-structuring and long-time-consuming collaborative project – whose returns are precisely so unimmediate, so precarious and so indirect.

I think of *Bouvard and Pécuchet* sitting on a bench by the Canal St Martin. Two new friends falling into friendship on a warm summer's evening. Marvelling over 'the catalogue of their shared tastes' (as Barthes puts it in *A Lover's Discourse*). This scene, affirms Barthes in Howard's translation, 'undoubtedly, is a love scene':

'You like this?'
(cinnamon, cold beer, lavender?)
'So do I!'
'You don't like that?'
(harpsichords, geraniums, women in trousers?)
'Neither do I!'

Two new friends making the decision to chuck in their careers as copyists and devote themselves to a new life of applied self-instruction. Where the digressive, frustrating path of the novel will be to move them out of the city to the countryside, into household management and smallholding and medicine and novel-writing, only to bring them back to exactly the position they started from: seated at a table copying out passages from other people's books. A path which makes no sense, really: they've learned nothing, earned nothing, accumulated nothing, apparently. But on the way there's been comedy, sunshine and companionship, argument and failure, literature and love.

I think of the researcher in the library, rereading *fifteen hundred books* originally read for the purposes of writing a comic novel about the failed application of books to life (even if she were capable of reading one whole book per day, with no breaks for weekends or holidays, the project would take her over four years to complete);

Of Robinson Crusoe desiring a table and having to fell –
having to waste the most part of – a whole tree in order to
smooth down each one of its solitary boards.

Then of the three years it took to complete the translation of a volume of lecture notes originally drafted in a matter of eight weeks. (My own way of expending my energy – *c'était ma depense à moi.*)

Robinson Crusoe is famously a novel of repetition, of doing and making things again: following the shipwreck, he remakes tools, re-cultivates crops, re-domesticates some kinds of animal, re-husbands others and eventually comes to re-enslave more people. But there is, of course, a crucial difference between so-called primitive man's path to civilization and the shipwrecked Robinson Crusoe. It is the difference between acting and re-enacting, between doing or making something for the very first time and knowingly redoing something that has already been done, or made, before.

For example, a table. There are already tables in the world. Robinson Crusoe knows this. But the point and his problem is: there are none *here*. Or none that he recognizes as being fully a table: only the flat-topped rocks that I imagine might have served him as an improvised writing and eating surface, or the stumps of fallen trees. He wants a *familiar* table, an Englishman's table, to act as the symbolic centre of his own home, his castle. He wants a table of the type that he has eaten off and written on before. Of the kind, indeed, that no one else here yet knows. No one, except perhaps the dogs and the cats. But not the parrot, and not Friday either, it seems, when he eventually appears. Introducing the table-from-England onto the island, with its powerful rectangular aesthetic, will be a way of transforming his new setting, of making a home there, of claiming, colonizing, a portion of the island-space. The way that sounds. At once so full of new possibility, because:

What will happen to the circle of the island when the table is imposed?

What different configurations of subject and space might its introduction produce?

Who will sit at it? What conversations will happen around it? What sorts of activities will its newly planed horizontal surface support?

A bit like the forest garden, transplanted in the mid-nineties into the heart of France's new national library. Will it *do* to lift a section of sycamore pines and transplant them here (I imagine the contractors asking themselves)? A rectangular-shaped section, sunk into the middle of a rectangular- (a page?-)shaped library, whose four corners are marked by four glass corner towers, standing, it is said, like upright half-open books. A rectangle of transplanted forest breathing in the heart of a library, surrounded by concrete and wood and glass, by a cinema now, and alongside the river. What new eco-systems will be formed among the books, the trees and the readers? Or between the readers coming here for the books and the communities making their homes in the surrounding residential buildings, distracted as they all sometimes are by the murmurations: the late autumn twilight spectacle of starlings rising and falling into the sycamore pines?

Projects so full of possibility, because we can't know. No one, I don't think, is in a position to know in advance what the remaking of a thing made (or grown) in one place in another – what Lawrence Venuti calls translation's necessary process of de- and re-contextualisation – will do.

(Since the inner garden was installed, the library's website tells me, a number of new trees have self-seeded themselves there by chance: nineteen cherrywoods, seven elderberries, three mountain ashes and one trembling poplar – also known as a quaking aspen.)

Projects that for precisely this reason are so risky and so perilous, because:

What indeed will happen?

When the Englishman makes his table again, with its imported aesthetic, only this time *here*, with the local materials and in the new setting of this wholly different island?

When he seats Friday at his table and starts speaking *at* him until he learns to speak back, instating a power dynamic, a learning relation, that is so entirely and so violently asymmetrical?

Or to the city birds, making new homes in the branches of imported trees, but getting regularly stunned now – knocked out – by the glass?

When it comes to making a table, Robinson Crusoe is

250

a novice, a beginner. He has never made a table before. But others have. He is fortunate in the sense that he has a model in mind: this, along with the many items he salvages from the ship (the tools, the grains, the gunpowder and the guns), is the embodied knowledge he carries with him. He knows what a table *is*: he has seen and used them before, back in York, England. Like the translator, he is not tasked – he has not tasked himself – with making something wholly original, in the sense of unprecedented, without reference or comparison. However it turns out, his table will not be an *invention*.

Which I realize is an altogether obvious point. But it is also the key, I think, to one of the further and very particular interests of writing a translation: 'As a temporary or permanent substitute for creation,' writes Simon Leys, in an essay translated by Dan Gunn, 'translation is closely allied to creation, and yet is of a different nature, for it offers an *artificial inspiration*.' He goes on: 'One can sit down at one's table every morning at the same hour, assured of giving birth to something. Of course, the quality and the quantity of daily production can vary, but the nightmare of the blank page is, for its part, definitively exorcised. It is, besides, this very reassuring guarantee which fundamentally places translation in the domain of the artisan rather than in that of the artist. However difficult translation may sometimes be, as distinct from creation it is fundamentally *risk-free*.'

When it comes to translation, and when it comes to what is specific and therefore specifically interesting about translation, there's never a question of *what* to write (and so, whether or not today there will be something to write) because the work has already been written. What matters is how to write it again.

Just make something up, is what Barthes said to Richard Howard. Just do whatever you want.

Can I? I've often wondered.

I've wanted to.

But then have found myself coming back round to thinking: if I *were* to just make something up, if I *were* to do whatever I wanted, would that not take me beside the point of writing a translation? In other words: would not making something (anything) up, doing *whatever* I wanted, mean writing something else? There's nothing to stop me, of course, from retroactively declaring my made-up or extrapolated or differently derived thing to be a translation, with all the performative power that the declaration *this is a translation* brings with it. And I have no intention of policing anyone else's power of naming, of limiting their expansion of what can be included in the genre-category of translation. But between myself and myself, I always seem to eventually come back round to thinking: the constraints on how far I can go, the limits on my making-up (because of course this is also what translation involves: making something, making this thing up again), the limits on doing what I want, are what *interest* me. They are what make the practice of translation specific and difficult and interesting in my experience of it. They interest me because they instruct me, leading me (forcing me?) outside of what I might already be capable of writing, thinking, knowing and imagining. I don't want to just make something up. Or perhaps elsewhere and one day I do. But I think I'll call it something else.

In an interview with Lydia Davis, Dan Gunn invites her to consider Leys's position. Do you agree? he asks. Do you *feel* substantially different when you are sitting down to write one of your stories, from how you feel when sitting down to 'translate' another chapter of *Bob, Son of Battle* (a novel for children first published in 1898 by Alfred Olivant, where Davis's project was to 'convert the Cumbrian and Scottish dialect – of which there is a huge amount – into clear standard English and to tinker throughout with the narrative passages so that the prose is less difficult.') Yes, says Davis, 'with just a slight hesitation at eliminating the idea of art from translation, at calling the translator an artisan or craftsperson rather than an artist. I say hesitation, not absolute refusal, because I generally have a two-fold reaction to the question of which exactly the translator is: first I want to say that the translator is more a highly skilled craftsperson than an artist, but then immediately think twice about it and feel that there are moments when real artistry is involved in translation.'

It is worth noting that, for Leys, the question of risk is related not to the event of translation – and thus to whether the translation will be good or bad, or what it might come to do in the world – but rather to the experience of writing something for the first time (of making something as yet unmade).

Davis goes on: 'To return to your question – it is true that the work to be done is already there in front of me when I sit down to translate; and that there is not the same risk involved as there is in creating a work of my own; and yes, I do feel different sitting down to a translation – whether from the French, or from the Dutch, or from *Bob, Son of Battle* – than I do sitting down to a story of my own.' However provisional and collapsible this distinction might be – and as, over the course of the interview, it proves to be (for instance, when Davis discusses her translations of the found Flaubert material that appear as new stories in her collection *Can't and Won't*), she insists on the possibility of making a distinction. The activities are related (they are very closely allied), but they are not *simply* the same.

I can think of a number of obvious ripostes to this. Perhaps the first would be to say: Yes but look. Look at all the writing that gets made from extant material and lays claim to the status of – and indeed operates as – new art.

And then to wonder out loud: Who was it that said the blank page is never blank, but always written over with quotations from existing works?

I could imagine a further objection which would begin by asking: Don't all writing projects involve working with existing rules and parameters that guide and to some degree direct what it is possible to write? And is this not, in its way, the lesson of the Oulipo? The *Ouvroir de littérature potentielle*, or workshop in potential literature, whose members, Georges Perec and Harry Mathews and Italo Calvino among them, were also fascinated practitioners of translation. The idea being that all writing is to some greater or lesser extent determined by constraints: the protocols of our literary genres (the seventeen syllables of the haiku; the rhetorical conventions of the academic essay; the shortness of a short story), as well as the operative rules of the language in which it is written. In recognition of this, the project of the Oulipo has been to invent and write under new constraints, as well as to reactivate old and forgotten ones (for instance the lipogram, the writing exercise which produced *La Disparition*, Perec's famous novel written without the letter e). The writing of translations is of special interest because it is especially directed and especially constrained; as such, this argument might go, it serves as an illuminating limit-case for all kinds of so-called spontaneous and undirected writing activity everywhere.

Yes, but – hold on.

To say all of that, I think, would be to pass too quickly over what is *not* the same about the project of making a translation.

To go too fast.

As Davis points out, the activities *are not simply* the same.

Because: come here, says the writing-to-be-translated. This is its invitation: come here, turn away from your blank page, your self-expression, your efforts at unprecedented monographic creation. Come here, sit down and attend for a while to this, to someone else's work, and let's see *what that* does. ('One of the ways to get around the confines of one's "identity" as one produces expository prose,' writes Spivak, 'is to work at someone else's title, as one works with a language that belongs to many others. This, after all, is one of the seductions of translating.')

Is it worth arguing over whether doing this, working at someone else's title, makes the translator a craftsperson rather than an artist? No, I don't think so. I'm not interested in thinking of art-making solely in terms of the first time, newness and invention. But I am interested in pushing a bit further at our understanding of craftsmanship, especially in relation to this question of risk.

In her recent book *The Argonauts* Maggie Nelson describes one of many and interchangeable long afternoons spent looking after her infant son. How she would observe him as he played on all fours in their backyard, contemplating 'which scraggly oak leaf to scrunch toward first with his dogged army crawl'. Observe him, sort of sprung. With the low-key primed alertness holding her ready to jump into action should ever she be required 'to harvest the leaf from his mouth'. The scene leads Nelson to make a direct address: 'You, reader,' she writes, 'are alive today, reading this, because someone once adequately policed your mouth exploring.'

Which is true. And at the same time nothing, as Nelson goes on to point out, to feel especially grateful for. So someone, someone who happened to be my own mum (but need not have been), once policed my mouth exploring. Nelson writes: 'Winnicott holds the relatively unsentimental position that we don't owe these people (often women, but by no means always) anything. But we do owe ourselves "an intellectual recognition of the fact that we were (psychologically) absolutely dependent, and that absolutely means absolutely. Luckily we were met by ordinary devotion."'

When my youngest son was a baby I had a bright hot technicolour dream that was the picture of him choking. This had the effect of elevating my adequate policing to the levels of nervous (paranoid?) surveillance. I'd hand him a slice of squashy ripe pear at lunch-time and watch as he'd try manoeuvring it delightedly into his mouth. Then suddenly doubt the size of it, the consistency of it, and to his great distress, whisk it away (I'm sorry, I'm sorry, I'm sorry! – don't cry: I'll cube it! Let me mash it!).

Looking back, I think what troubled me the most was the thought (the thought and also the reality) that the smallest lapse in my attention, even (even and especially) with respect to the most ordinary everyday things – eating a pear for lunch, sitting out among the dry leaves in the garden – could have consequences on this other, life-or-death scale. The stakes felt everywhere and for that period of time almost unbearably high.

The further analogy I seem to be on my way to proposing is a bit (or indeed entirely) unfitting. I'll force it nevertheless. In the first place because policing my son's mouth exploring and writing the Barthes translations coincided for a while in my own life's activities. But then for the more considered reason that this acute sense of minute-by-minute and yet at the same time altogether commonplace and everyday *risk* says something about what's at stake in the project of writing a translation, especially when it is conceived in terms of *making a whole*.

In *The Nature and Art of Workmanship,* an important treatise first published in the late 1960s, David Pye offers new
terms for thinking about and valuing the objects we think
of as having their basis in craft. When we speak of craft,
he says, we normally tend to mean something hand- as
distinct from machine-made, or something made singly
rather than mass-produced. But in fact, as Pye shows,
these distinctions are not especially useful or tenable.
Many things made by hand also involve the use of tools
(and when is a tool not a machine?); a workman may well
switch from working by hand to working with machines
within the same job. What's more, there's no necessary or
constitutive value in something having been made singly:
clearly it's very useful to be able to make multiple things at
once, and mass-produced objects are often very beautiful.
(Among the black-and-white photographs illustrating
Pye's book, one shows an ornate nineteenth-century
drawing-room cabinet made by Holland and Sons, currently held in the collections of the V&A. On the facing
page is a beer-can shot from above, with its old-style
ring-pull still intact. The latter being an example of such
excellent workmanship, observes Pye, that 'any true
craftsman would feel something of a pang at throwing it
away'.) No, a better and more meaningful distinction, he
argues, one which provides more meaningful grounds for
valuing the qualities we usually associate with craftsmanship ('diversity', 'durability' and 'equivocality'), pertains
not to different classes of object but to two different kinds
of workmanship. The distinction is this: on the one hand,
there is the kind of workmanship 'where the quality of
the result is exactly predetermined before a single thing
is made'. This is the kind to be found 'in quantity production, and found in its pure state in pure automation'.
It is altogether useful and expedient; its products – like

lightbulbs, for instance, or a ring-pull – are of value and can be beautiful precisely because they are uniformly made. Let's call this 'the workmanship of certainty'. On the other is the kind of workmanship which might *also* use a whole range of machines and tools and templates and what Pye calls 'shape-determining jigs,' but with the difference that here the outcome depends far more on the 'judgement, dexterity and care which the maker exercises as he works'. In this case, the 'essential idea' is that the 'quality of the result is not pre-determined [but] continually at risk during the process of making'. For this reason, says Pye, I'll call the second form of workmanship 'the workmanship of risk' – where, 'the risk of spoiling the job,' he stresses, is 'at every minute real'.

Here is George Orwell again, writing this time in *The Road to Wigan Pier* and dreaming, now, of tables: 'Here am I working eight hours a day in an insurance office; in my spare time I want to do something "creative", so I choose to do a bit of carpentering – to make myself a table, for instance. Notice from the very start that there's a touch of artificiality about the whole business, for the factories can turn me out a table far better than one I can make for myself. But even when I get to work on my table, it is not possible for me to feel towards it as the cabinet-maker of a hundred years ago felt towards his table, still less as Robinson Crusoe felt towards his.'

But why not? Why does Orwell feel so sure of not feeling for his projected table what Robinson Crusoe must have fictionally felt towards his? Because, it would seem, making a table 'nowadays' is as alienated an activity as working in an insurance office. There's no judgement and no dexterity, no skill and no creativity. Not even any 'creativity'. Orwell's complaint being that everything, every stage in the process, has been more or less decided for him in advance. He writes: 'before I start, most of the work has already been done for me by machinery. The tools I use demand the minimum of skill. I can get, for instance, planes which will cut out any moulding; the cabinet-maker of a hundred years ago would have had to do the work with chisel and gouge, which demanded real skill of eye and hand. The boards I buy are ready planed and the legs are ready turned by the lathe. I can even go to the wood-shop and buy all the parts of the table ready-made and only needing to be fitted together; my work being reduced to driving in a few pegs and using a piece of sandpaper. And if this is so at present, in the mechanized future it will be enormously more so.' It is not just, then, that we tend to take a great deal of care over the things (the writing or the people) we feel something for. An extended time frame of care which need not always, of course, involve very much at all: just being there, doing the things that need to be done ('ordinary devotion'). What I also take from this is the idea that individuated judgement and dexterity, skill and creativity, together with the kinds of qualities that we note and want to preserve in our age of increased mechanization, as well as the kinds of feelings that Orwell wants to feel, come into play (only?) when the outcomes of our activities are not already wholly predetermined. When, that is, and however apparently commonplace or uncreative the

264

activity, there is still and always a real-life risk – which is to say, when you are repeatedly and at every minute having to face down the real-life risk – of irreversibly and irretrievably fucking it up.

Look to the whole, the translator asked.

The line comes from Helen Lowe-Porter's correspondence, and can be read as an early plea (from a letter to her publisher Alfred A. Knopf, dated 11 November 1943) against the kind of translation review which proceeds by finding and scrutinizing the apparent lapse, the moments of inattention, the local mistake or infelicity – which might always be of the order of a conscious decision on the translator's part – and making these stand in for the quality of the full translation. Michelle Woods discusses this very common form of translation-evaluation in the section titled 'Gotcha!' of her account of Kafka's English-language translators and translations. The expression comes from the translator Mark Harman, whose 1998 translation of Kafka's *The Castle* was widely reviewed and discussed. In this kind of review, as Woods writes, 'reviewers often hone in on perceived "mistakes" in order to justify their own taste preferences and to present their own legitimacy as experts in judging a translation. Rarely glimpsed is a consideration of the translator, or where translation fits into their career and their background ... and what the nature of their contribution should be.' Looking to the whole is a call to consider the way the thing is working and reading altogether, the way its many parts work in relation to one another, and the larger ways in which the translation relates to the circumstances and motivations for making it (a call that, as Woods points out, Lawrence Venuti makes repeatedly throughout his work).

I would agree: it is unhelpful and unrealistic to think that a translation could fail as the result of a single or sample of local mistakes. For one thing, as Pye also points out, there is clearly a great deal more to making –to writing, to translation (to childcare?) – than not 'spoiling the job'.

According to Pye, a more productive set of criteria for evaluating the quality of workmanship – more productive than the commonly used 'good' and 'bad', 'precise' and 'rough' – would be 'soundness' and 'comeliness'. Soundness, he writes, implies 'the ability to transmit and resist forces', while comeliness 'the ability to give the aesthetic expression which the designer [standing in here for the first writer] intended'. Or, indeed, 'to add to it'. He goes on: 'in some cases precision is necessary to soundness, but in many others it is not, and rough workmanship will do the job just as well. In some cases precision is necessary to the intended aesthetic expression but in others it is not and, on the contrary, rough workmanship is essential to it.' Not good or bad, then, nor precise or rough, not smooth or awkward, but sound or comely.

Soundness: the idea being that you should be able to *use* the thing made, to read it, to write on it, to drop it, to push at bits of it, to cite others, to set it to work and to activate it in all these ways in the context of your own life – and still it would hold. Comeliness: pleasing in its features and its proportions.

I'm not sure how much work these new criteria could be made to do in the evaluation of translations. But I like them (I offer them here as possibilities to think on).

It is unhelpful to presume that a translation could fail as the result of a single or sample of local mistakes: gotcha! Thinking that it *might* is the mindset of the reviewers gamely offering their own corrections for the local scrutinized part. But it is also – is it not? – the mindset of the translator, with her constant attentiveness, the very close form of her attention, her overall care. Or, to put the point another way, I think we owe translators, and perhaps also ourselves as readers of translations, not gratitude, but rather *some intellectual recognition of the fact* that her work pertains not just to this or that part picked out for late scrutiny by the reader or the reviewer, but to *every single one of the small parts* forming the whole. In other words: I think we owe translators, and perhaps also ourselves, some recognition of what it might have meant *to have handled every single word* (space and punctuation mark) of the writing-to-be-translated, *to have taken a decision in relation to* its every single word (space and punctuation mark), and indeed *to have written* every single one of its parts, where those parts are recognized to be the combinatory elements of its larger discursive structures (paragraphs, chapters, the whole thing), and where *each and every one of its parts* is another way of saying *each and every one of its questions*, every single one of the questions, of every kind of order, that the project of translating causes to emerge (answers formulated in the form of a new sentence; then, a great sequence of new sentences), which might in turn be another way of saying *each and every one of its risks*. Risks which are if not quite *at every moment* (since early decisions can of course be considered and considered and edited and reconsidered) then certainly in every detail *real*.

For example: do we *write* translations or do we *make* them? Or, indeed, do we *do* them? It's a question that setting the practice of translation in relation to tables, to craft and workmanship was always going to raise. It also pertains to one of my own local translation decisions. A decision that wasn't made spontaneously, not off-the-cuff or in the moment, but reflected upon and discussed with others and reconsidered – and then upheld nonetheless. The decision was to translate, in more or less every instance where Barthes, in the last lecture course, uses the verb *faire* (to do or to make), the verb as 'writing' or 'to write'. '*Comment faire un roman*?' Barthes asks himself and his audience. How to *make* a novel? (would be an alternative translation). And: Will I really *make* one? My feeling now is that this was a mistake. The choice of *faire* rather than *écrire* in Barthes's lectures opens writing up to other proximate forms of doing and making, not least the activity of the dressmaker at her table, piecing together her bits and pieces of material. It is also its own way of repeatedly insisting on the central concerns of the course which, says Barthes, were practical writing matters. Matters of how-to-write (how to make or do) a novel and not what-is-a-novel. There is a difference, he maintains, between wanting to know what something *is* and wanting to know *how something was made* in order to make it or do it again and it is the second kind of knowledge, says Barthes, that concerns us here (just as it is this second kind of knowledge that is of concern to the translator and, I would suggest, is produced by her activity). Will they interest you? he asks. These technical writing questions, will they interest you? The audience he was addressing, in the late 1970s, was not the audience of the contemporary creative writing workshop. Will you be interested, asks Barthes, in what he also calls these 'humble' problems of writing technique? I mean, there's a real risk that you might not: those among you who don't write, who have no writing fantasy of your own. But my hope is you will, he says. A hope that rests on personal experience. Because, the fact of the matter is, I personally never tire of people telling me about their work – the word he uses is *métier* – the problems of their craft, no matter what it is they do. Unfortunately, as we all know, people always feel somehow obliged to engage in *general conversation* (which is always an intense field of censorship). How often have I felt irritated, exasperated by a conversation with some specialist – a doctor, a plumber – which has been made *general*. When I would have loved – how much would I have loved! – to hear him talk about his specialism. But I'm offered banalities! Intellectuals in particular never talk about their craft. It's as if they didn't really have one, as if the term didn't pertain to them: they have ideas, positions, with no craft! What I am calling 'technique, the technical' in writing, says Barthes, is basically the experience of writing itself. That is, as I, the translator, understand it: the engaging with it, the actual experience of doing it. An experience, he claims, that is always 'moral and humble'. This is where technical and – to the extent that the technical aspects of writing are always directed towards, always aspiring to an aesthetic – aesthetic concerns intersect with the ethical aspects of writing. Says Barthes, I want this lecture course to be situated 'at the intersection between the Aesthetic and the Ethical'.

Is this true, I wonder, as I try translating and retranslating this passage? Is it true that the lived experience of writing is always necessarily humbling (and therefore in some way 'moral', 'ethical')?

Moral, perhaps, in the sense that Barthes gives to 'modest', or 'non-arrogant'. I'm reminded of Barthes's lecture titled '*Longtemps je me suis couché de bonne heure*' in which he first formulates his desire for a novel and points to Proust as a model. Given the title, should we expect this lecture to be *on* Proust? Barthes asks out loud. Yes and no. The actual topic will be – if you will, says Barthes, if you'll indulge me on this: Proust and me. Sounds presumptuous, I know. Nietzsche spared no irony on the Germans' use of that conjunction. Schopenhauer *and* Hartmann, he would jeer. *Really*? Proust and me, says Barthes, sounds even worse (the link it makes, the connection it presumes, is even bolder). And yet, he goes on. In making this association between myself and Proust, by putting us both on the same level in this way, the point is – once again, the note of caution – not to *compare* myself to a great writer, but rather to affirm, in a very different manner, that *I identify with him*: confusion of *practice*, not of value. Let me explain, says Barthes: in figurative literature, in the novel, for example, it seems true to say that we identify with one of the characters represented (I mean, intermittently, for stretches of our reading if not throughout). This projection, I believe, is one of the animating forces, the wellsprings of literature; but in some marginal cases, in the case, for example, of the reader who has writerly ambitions of his own, the reading subject no longer identifies exclusively with one or other of the characters represented. He also, and principally, identifies with the author of the book he is reading, for the reason that the author must have wanted to write this work and has clearly succeeded. Now, Proust is the privileged site of this peculiar form of identification, since *In Search of Lost Time* is the narrative of a desire to write: I'm not identifying with the prestigious author of a monumental work of literature, says Barthes, I'm identifying with the writer-as-*labourer* – now tormented, now exalted, but in all events *modest* –

271

How to *make* a novel? The emphasis on making – the verb *faire* opening up a space for making as well as writing, for writing-as-making, writing-as-technique, as craftsmanship – is a way of holding the project at a distance from the mythology of the writer: the published writer for whom the work is done (consecrated, the writer and his work monumentalized). It is a way of holding it still open and mobile, as a practice that Barthes, or indeed his audience could share in, too. The idea that the labour of writing is necessarily modest, humble, might be to replace one myth with another. But it also speaks back to Barthes's investment in the amateur, in her own form of expending energy, the ways in which she chooses, repeatedly, and with investment, to spend her time. What is he, what is she doing? In her drawing room? At the piano? She too is playing, she too is making something, she too is writing. Her gestures are of the same order as the professional's. These are activities that she too finds time for within the space and among the competing demands of her life, and does so every day. For me, says Barthes, the place where this alliance occurs, where the aesthetic (as the vocation of the technical) meets the ethical – its privileged field – is precisely here: in what he calls the everyday detail of the domestic setting, the home. This is my fantasy, he says, this is the mode of writing I am projecting for myself: a domestic working practice, working from home, which would also entail the writing of the small differences among the days. Hence, once again, the interest in the haiku, which to Barthes's mind has the capacity to do exactly this: a mode of recording the incidents of daily life, its particularities, the fragile and short-lived reach of the relations between the subject and the world that each tiny poem describes. For Barthes, attending to the detail of domestic life in no way implied a narrowing or circumscribing of the field of interest. On the contrary, as Adrienne Ghaly argues: in the lectures on the haiku, especially, this technical-ethical question of *how* indeed to write (how to make, how to produce) these '"thin" or minimalist relations to the world' – *how*, exactly, one might go about doing this, engaging with the actuality, the real-life practice of doing this – is, for Barthes, a way of asking about 'language's power to disrupt dominating, classifying and appropriating stances to which certain kinds of language use commit us'. It is a way of asking how to write (and thus also how to make?) the world differently.

There's an essay by Paul Valéry called 'Variations on the *Eclogues*', published in a translation by Denise Folliot in 1953, which has something to say about the modesty in making: this idea that there might be something inherently levelling about making concrete things. It also speaks of translation explicitly in terms of volume-approximation – as directed by the concern to reproduce the *whole* insofar as it is materially possible for the translator to do so, attending to the detail of its every part, as well as to how altogether it takes up space. The scenario is this: Valéry has been asked by a friend to translate Virgil's *Eclogues*, also known as the *Bucolics*, from Latin into French. But because the friend intends to produce what in French is called *un beau livre*, a beautiful-looking, often expensively produced book, there is a layout concern. He wants the pages to be 'well-balanced'. And so 'decided it would be well if the Latin and French were to correspond line for line'. A line for a line, a page for a page. Now the difficulty with this, Valéry explains, is that Latin is in general 'a more compact language' than French: it is, as he puts it, 'chary of auxiliaries'; it is 'sparing of prepositions'. It can say 'the same things with fewer words' and, moreover, is able to arrange these 'with enviable freedom'. 'The Latin poet, working within the wide bounds of his syntax can do more or less as he likes'; the French poet, on the other hand 'does what he can within the very narrow bounds of his own'.

The concern to approximate the original form line by line, writing a new line for each one of its lines, is what prompts – because it is bound up with – this further inquiry into the expressive possibilities of each language. The way, for example, English, with its precise single-word verbs (to cuddle, to eavesdrop), is also said to be a more economical language than French (if I were to cuddle you in French I would – more wordily – *te faire un calin,* or *te prendre dans mes bras*; if I were to eavesdrop on you I would *écouter tes conversations privées*, maybe, or *t'écouter d'une façon indiscrète*). The translator of Western languages has to contend with these general quantitative differences – what it is possible to say in what quantity of words – as well as, of course, with the particular expressive economy of the writer she is undertaking to translate.

Enfin bref, Barthes writes, sometimes, in the lecture notes.

A small verbal gesture. Marking a change, an end and a new beginning, in the way a conductor uses a hand to swallow the end of a note.

Enfin bref.

The difficulty of doing (making, writing) something of the same subtle order in a comparable number of words:

So, anyway.

There we have it.

For Valéry, as well as the economic differences (what it is possible to say in what quantity of words) between Latin and French, there was the further problem of feeling underqualified. Nothing marked me out for the translation project, he writes (the modesty of a celebrated poet, Chair of Poetics from 1937 to 1945 at the Collège de France): I hardly knew any Latin: my small amount of schoolboy's Latin had faded, after fifty-five years, to a memory of a memory.

I hardly knew anything about Virgil.

Who am I to attempt the *Bucolics*, when so many men, so scholarly and erudite, have toiled over three or four centuries at the translation of them?

What's more, bucolic themes don't interest me.

Pastoral life is quite foreign to me and strikes me as tedious.

I get depressed by the sight of furrows.

The recurrence of the seasons depresses me, also, showing only the stupidity of nature and life, which can persist only by repeating themselves.

I shall confess that I was born in a port.

No fields round about, only sand and salt water.

And yet in the end I accepted the commission. For the fact is, he writes, I am compliable; my habit is to give in to fate, to chance. Because it is my conviction that no one knows what he is doing or what he will become. And so again I opened my school Virgil. And, after a while, he writes, as I went on with my translation, making, unmaking, remaking, sacrificing here and there, restoring (as best I could) what I had first rejected – this labour of approximation, with its little successes, its regrets, its conquests and its resignations, produced in me an interesting feeling. (Of which I was not immediately aware.)

The sensation was of 'a poet at work'.

Here am I, writes Valéry, at my desk, with a famous book, set in its millennial fame.

And here I am *arguing* with it.

Arguing with it as freely as if it were a poem of my own on the table before me.

In the process of translating it, the set book – once fixed in its fame, *these* necessary words in *this* necessary order – starts to unsettle. The immobile poem gets sort of remobilized; each of its necessary lines looking now like a sequence of decisions, or indeed of accidents, made by a writing subject engaged in a similar kind of activity. Interestingly, this sensation of the poet at work, with its levelling effect – the labour of two writers at their desks, writing at very different times, in different ways (the one writing something on the close basis of what the other once produced) but both *writing* nevertheless – opens out onto a new boldness. If this indeed were once written, a reality that I am able to fully recognize only now that I too am writing it – only now that I find myself engaged in the complex process of writing it again – then why should I not argue with you? Why should my writerly instincts, my different ideas and my own particular aesthetic, necessarily cleave to yours?

These are the questions Valéry finds himself asking.

At times, he notes, as I worked on my translation, I caught myself wanting to change something in the venerable text. This lasted for one or two seconds of actual time and amused me.

Why not?

I said to myself, returning from this short absence:

Why not?

Because this, I think, is the nature of the relation. This is its asymmetry, or what Anita Raja, in her lecture titled 'Translation as a Practice of Acceptance' calls its 'inequality'. As a translator, however collaborative I consider my process to be, however much my writing, my thinking, depends on and is so closely directed by yours – indeed, the fact is, it couldn't exist without it – at the end of the day (at the very end of all the days it can take to translate a long work), I am responsible for you. I am responsible for you; not you for me. (Preparing food for my son to eat, if the slice of pear turns out to be too big for him to comfortably swallow, then that will have been my fuck-up and not his.) This is what I take on. This is what shapes my response to the question 'Why not?' each time it arises (a response that has to be each time newly configured in relation to the new circumstances in which it arises). I can't *just* make something up. I can't *just* change something in the 'venerable' text, and replace it with something invented of my own.

Meanwhile, of course, within the parameters of the project I have taken on and in response to the instruction of the sentence I am undertaking to translate – its detailed constraints – this is exactly what I'm doing: changing, replacing. I'm never *simply* making something up but I am nevertheless making something (something new in the name of againness). I accept this peculiar writing scenario – I willingly accept it. Although I don't think it would be true to say that I accept or have ever accepted it once and for all. I don't think I could claim to be capable of accepting this and my acceptance holding once and for all. Which is how I understand the title of Raja's lecture: translation as 'a practice of acceptance': an ongoing practice of acceptance, an ongoing rethinking, readjusting and reaccepting the terms of my acceptance.

Translators must write and thereby attend to the whole.

Translators must write and thereby attend to the whole.

But have I fully stated, yet, why this matters?

I think of the kind of materialized reading practice performed by a guy whom Barthes once sat next to on a bus. The number 21 bus, crowded, a Sunday evening in July. This guy, as Barthes tells it, who was engaged in underlining – conscientiously, with a ruler and a black Biro – 'every single one of the lines' in the book he was reading. In other words, the whole book. Why? Presumably because everything – every bit of it – mattered. Nothing could be reasonably or responsibly left out.

Likewise, translation. An obvious point, perhaps, but again one that is worth stating and restating, if only because this is one of the further constraints that distinguishes translation from the many other processes and practices with which it is often compared (into which it is so often collapsed). A translation can't really be, at least not in principle, *a great deal* shorter or smaller than the original. It can't really leave things out. Although of course there have been translations across the history of literary translation that miss things, that excise and abridge things and function as and are considered translations nevertheless. Consider an example discussed by Lawrence Venuti: Abbé Prévost's French version of *Pamela*, which reduced the seven English volumes to four in French. Even so, Prévost declared: 'I have not changed anything pertaining to the author's intention ... nor have I changed much in the manner in which he put that intention into words.' Or, a mid-twentieth-century example: take the first English version of Simone de Beauvoir's *The Second Sex* by Howard M. Parshley, published in 1953, which cut fifteen per cent of the original's 972 pages. Or the poet Paul Legault's recent English-to-English translations of Emily Dickinson's complete poems where, instead of approximating the size, the sometimes already minute volume, of the original poems, his translations are always and deliberately much shorter (one-liners). These examples are interesting, I think, not because they show how flexible this constraint really is, how infrequently it has been adhered to, but because, in their provocation, they show up the degree to which we feel, generally speaking, that it should be. Three volumes of the novel not translated? Crucial chapters missing? A fourteen-line poem made again as a one-liner? The feeling is: that can't be right. That can't really be a translation in the 'proper' sense of the term. Perhaps what we're dealing with here is something generically different – some proximate but *not altogether identical* practice with its own, different history and protocol: the abridgement; the précis.

That said, just as a translation can't, in principle, be *a great deal* shorter or smaller than the original material in quantitative terms, nor can it be *a great deal* longer or bigger. This is the point that Jacques Derrida makes in a lecture on literary and philosophical translation. And it strikes me as true: I feel this to be true, and once again the exceptions serve only to confirm the feeling. In Lawrence Venuti's translation, Derrida offers the following scenario: imagine, he writes, a translator who is 'fully competent in at least two languages and two cultures, two cultural memories with the sociohistorical knowledge embodied in them. Now give her all the time in the world, as well as all the words needed to explicate, clarify and teach the semantic content and forms of the text.' Give her 'an entire book filled with translator's notes', he suggests, and there is really no reason why she should 'fail to render – without any remainder – the intentions, meaning, denotations, connotations and semantic over-determinations, the semantic effects of what is called the original'. Give her a big enough book – enough space and enough time (a lifetime) – and she should be in a position to render them all. A translator like Vladimir Nabokov, for example, who famously materialized his dream of a translation with footnotes rising up the page like skyscrapers in an edition of Pushkin's *Eugene Onegin* ('I want translations with copious footnotes, footnotes reaching up like skyscrapers to the top of this or that page so as to leave only the gleam of one textual line between commentary and eternity.'). Yes, fine. And why not? What an extraordinary project (David Damrosch notes how in 'Nabokov's *Onegin* the actual poem takes up only one seventh of the edition's fourteen hundred pages.'). The only problem with such an undertaking, following Derrida's argument, is that 'this operation, which occurs daily in the university and in literary criticism, is not what is called translation, a translation worthy of the name, a translation in the strict sense, the translation of a work'. In its length, its excessive expansion and additional over-length, it has become something else: translation *plus* commentary, criticism, explanation, gloss, scholarship.

It is not my intention to hold anyone to making translations in the 'strict', 'proper' or 'standard' sense (all those adjectives are inadequate), nor is it to suggest that translation *doesn't* or in some way *can't* also involve reading, synthesis, synopsis, criticism, explanation, gloss, scholarship. Translations very often *are* somewhat longer than the originals, they come with their own additional contextualizing textual apparatus (my translations of the lectures, for example, includes a translator's preface, situating Barthes's work). It's more to try to register what happens – the special kind of knowledge that gets produced – when the concern is to write the whole, when someone endeavours to reproduce, more or less (with all the differences that writing the thing again in a new language makes), a given work's economy of expression. Or, in other words, how the work is saying what it is saying and doing what it is doing in its given number of words, with its punctuation, white space and use of larger discursive structures. How, working with the constraint of the whole, the practice of translation is also a way of attending to and thinking about this economy in terms of form. A short form for a short form. A long form for a long form. A pithy sentence for a pithy one. A line for a line. The work of translation, as Valéry affirms, always involves 'a certain approximation of form'. Where form means genre as well as size and shape and duration and volume: the way the writing-to-be-translated unfolds, the way it is paced, the way it reads over time together with the way it has been shaped and the way that shape occupies space, engages with and configures the spaces around it. This kind of materialized attending to happens at the level of the sentence, the smaller part, the local move or gesture that the translator works to reproduce in her own setting, with her own body and her own different materials. It also happens – what interests me about translation is the way it must also happen – at the level of the whole. A whole newly produced and differently inscribed in its different surroundings, existing *here* now,

    where it didn't before.

Like what?

Like a table.

Like an Englishman's rectangular table made again for the first time

in the circle of undeserted island.

I set the comparison down – I have been using it – as a device to think with. A comparison; yet another possible and limitedly illuminating metaphor for translation.

There have been so many.

There's a panel discussion you can watch on YouTube, a *London Review of Books* event on translating Kafka, where Anthea Bell, the celebrated translator from the German, French and Danish, describes once trying very hard to talk about her work in concrete terms, without making an image out of it. It was in conversation with the winner of a book prize, she recalls: a very good Italian author; very fluent in English. They were discussing the translation process and she proposed to try saying something about it without recourse to metaphor.

You see, she said, it's like this: after the first reading, that particularly close, intensive reading that for me is the preliminary stage for all translation, the translator's mind dwells somewhere, for a little while, in a place where there isn't any language at all.

And then, with luck, she comes down with an English draft.

The young Italian writer received her description, thought about it. Then turned to her good-humouredly and asked: okay, but tell me. Where exactly – where concretely, that is, where literally – is this place you're talking about?

And she laughed, because of course she realized what she'd done.

I set the table down as a metaphor; or, more precisely, as an analogy.

An analogy, of course, is a special kind of comparison. It has the features of an argument, and is usually made for the purposes of clarification or explanation. It works by pointing to something familiar or readily understood in order to clarify or explain something more complex and less readily understood. If the analogy is a good one then it should last long enough for the complex thing to be clarified or explained: for it to emerge, instructively, that *this* is indeed a bit like *that*.

But not only does its good functioning depend on knowing which of the two terms is the simpler and which is the more complex – in this case, table-making or translating? – it is also in the very nature of the analogy that at some point it will break down: the ways in which *this*, in fact, now you or I come to think of it, is actually quite unlike *that*, will always win out, eventually.

Shall I break it down now?

I read *Robinson Crusoe* for the purposes of translating Barthes's first lecture course.

In fact I reread it; I had read it before, but had forgotten most of it (all of the long second part: who remembers the wolves?!).

I remember reading the passage about making a table, and thinking and feeling very strongly that this account of remaking a familiar thing – of so laboriously remaking an existing thing – *knew* something about the practice of translation.

I recently went back and read it for the third time.

And discovered – reading more concentratedly this time? – that the infinitely laborious method, the one whereby a whole tree makes but one solitary board, actually describes how Robinson Crusoe made some shelves. The table, on the other hand, he knocked together with bits of ready-made plank. The passage I quoted continues:

'When I had wrought out some boards, as above, I made large shelves of the breadth of a foot and a half, one over another, all along one side of the cave, to lay all my tools, nails and ironwork, and in a word, to separate everything at large in their places, that I might easily come at them; I knocked pieces into the wall of the rock to hang my guns and all things that would hang up.

However I made me a table and chair, as I observed above, in the first place, and this I did out of the short pieces of boards that I brought on my raft from the ship.'

It was a mistake, a misreading. Of the kind that happens when you bring your own agenda, your own desire, your own ideas to a book, however much you might want to learn from and be instructed by it. In other words, of the kind that happens in reading and translating. It made sense to me that it should be a table, and not shelves, that he spent such a long time making. In the same way as it made sense to Orwell that Robinson Crusoe should feel something for his table and not for his shelves; that the novel should become interesting only at the point which he starts making a table – precisely, a table, and not any of the other objects he undertakes to make. I imagine this has to do with the way tables have so often been used as devices to think with.

Philosophy, observes Sara Ahmed, is full of tables, full of examples of tables (of tables – writing desks especially – being invoked as examples). Though perhaps this is not altogether surprising: tables, after all, 'are "what" philosophy is written upon'. When reaching for a concrete example of an object, something solid, something familiarly real, something that is very and indisputably *there* and, no doubt, within reach, philosophers have very often reached for the table. When explaining how a wholly useful thing acquires new value the moment it is exchanged Marx, too, points to a table. The famous wooden table: the basic elementarily useful thing that grimaces and gurns, grow paws and a tail, and sets itself upright to dance the strange seductive dance of the commodity. It was Derrida, who at one point looks up from his close reading of this passage in Marx's *Capital* to survey 'all the tables' that have appeared in what he calls our – Western, male, almost exclusively white European – 'patrimony'. So many, he writes, 'that we have lost count of them, in philosophy, rhetoric, poetics, from Plato to Heidegger, from Kant to Ponge, and so many others'.

'Think of a kitchen table ... when you're not there,' Andrew Ramsay suggests to Lily Briscoe in Virginia Woolf's *To the Lighthouse*, as part of an effort to explain his father's philosophy of subject and object and the nature of reality. The kitchenyness of the table, its multipurpose-ness, suggesting that perhaps thinking has always happened, and is currently still happening, on that kind of surface, too.

So many tables, acting as so many *supports* for the ideas we receive.

I am attached to my misreading, I realize. Inspired by the way Oana Avasilichioaei and Erín Moure run the word 'translation' through all the possible dictionary definitions and common sayings pertaining to 'roof' (noun and verb) in their work *Expeditions of a Chimaera* – an exercise which produces such newly phrased and newly proffered idioms as 'to hit the translation' (to become very angry) and 'to have a translation over one's head' (to have somewhere to live) and 'to be under a person's translation' (to be in a person's home) – I turn stubbornly to the dictionary, determined to think whatever else my table analogy will give me cause to think. It produces this:

If a translation is like a table, then it consists of a flat slab-like top braced by legs or other (normally, but not always, visible) supports.

And if to translate is to table, then this means to submit for consideration, to propose, as well as to suspend consideration indefinitely.

If a translation is like a table, then it has known and is open to different kinds of making (for example, both its initial assemblage and its later repeated setting).

If a translation is like a table, then one way of earning a living – meagre, maybe, but intellectually challenging and advantageously flexible – is to wait them. As in: she worked her way through the baby years by waiting trans-lations. (*American usage*)

If a translation is like a table, then it is also, etymologically speaking, a plate, a meal, an offering.

If a translation is like a table, then it is either, or can be alternately, the thing itself and the configuration of persons and relations around it.

In the terms of my misreading, the problem Robinson Crusoe sets himself is how to make a table in what for him will be for the first time, in his new, unlikely circumstances. And the crucial, final point is this: the methods that might have been used to make the tables he has seen, eaten and worked at before are radically unavailable to him now. It is the total unavailability of those original methods – not only because he is not a natural craftsman but also because, even if he were, his setting, his resources, his new materials are very different – that makes his problem so interesting and still, to my mind, so very translation-like. There can be no question of Robinson Crusoe making a table *in the same way* as the tables he has eaten off or written on at his father's house, back in York, England. The project involves coming up with his own idiosyncratic solution to the problem of making through the effort of practically engaging with it. A project that demands both *application* and *contrivance*. Thus, he writes: 'I made abundance of things even without tools, and some with no more tools than an adze and a hatchet, which were perhaps *never made that way before*.'

Likewise, I contrived to write two volumes of Barthes's lecture notes again in English. And although at that point they had already been translated (for example, from the French into German by Horst Brühmann in 2008, under the title *Die Vorbereitung des Romans* or from the French into Italian by Emiliana Galiani and Julia Ponzio, whose *La preparazione del romanzo* was published in 2010), I can assert with confidence that *they have never been made in that way before.*

Notes for lectures that were drafted at relative speed, with a fountain pen, in various inks (blue and red and green), marked by crossings out, underlinings, with margin notes and new passages attached to the pages by paper clip, over summer weeks spent at the house in Urt, a village in the South-West of France.

Notes for the lectures that were then delivered in the mid- to late 1970s in the setting of the Collège de France: one lecture a week between December 1976 and May 1977 for *Comment vivre ensemble*, between February and June 1978 for *Le Neutre* and December 1978 and March 1980 for *La préparation du roman.*

Lectures whose live delivery was recorded and archived.

Notes for the lectures that came eventually to be edited, more than twenty years later, under the general direction of Éric Marty. And, for the two courses I translated, the editorship of Claude Coste for *Comment vivre ensemble*, and Nathalie Léger for *La préparation du roman I et II.* Notes that were then copy-edited, made into a book (published in Seuil's *Traces écrites* series, with its specifically plain, cahier-like design) in French in 2003.

Books that I bought that year, I think, or the one after, in a bookshop on the rue des Écoles.

Audio recordings that would be made available for purchase at around the same time.

In 2016, a new edition of *La préparation du roman* would be published. Based not on a transcription of Barthes's notes – his score for the performance of the lectures – but the recordings themselves. A new version which reads altogether differently: in place of the stop-start, telegrammatic quality is transcribed, unpausing speech – which, provocatively, makes for a writing so much closer to the kind of ongoing, continuous prose Barthes dreamt of for his novel. A new commodity which looks entirely different from the first version: now there is a handsome black-and-white photograph of Barthes on the cover (one of the reasons given for publishing the course again, repackaged, in this new, more 'readable' version, so relatively soon after the first plain edition, is because 'it didn't find its readership' – it didn't sell many copies? – the first time around).

The labour of translation – working the lecture notes into English on a PC on my table by the window some forty years after their original drafting, as well as that of the readers I consulted, the copy-editors, the managing editor, the designers who collaborated on the production of these new books, with their bold design and shiny covers – was *different*.

A question Ahmed asks in her discussion of philosophy's tables: 'What work goes into the making of things, such that they take form as this thing or that thing?'

Perhaps, once again, the point is so self-evident that it doesn't bear making. Except that not only does the translator's method differ from the first writer's, for the reasons that Leys and Davis gave, to do with the difference between what it is to invent something for the first time and the very specific project of writing an existing thing again. It will also each time differ, as it were, from itself. The basic instruction, the genre-defining constraint that makes a translation a translation is to write the writing again in another language. And I could tell you that this is indeed more or less what I do every time I translate, and more or less what anyone does every time they undertake to translate, whatever it is that they are translating, and from whatever languages they are translating from and into, and this would be true, but only because it is so broadly, loosely unspecific. In order to work some specificity, some of my own-particular-case idiosyncrasy into it, I could tell you how I proceeded in the most general sense: how I would begin by writing a first English draft of the lecture courses, highlighting in yellow everything I was as yet undecided about until the screen was ablaze with it: a Word doc like a rapeseed field in flower. How I would go through the draft again and again, revising, reading it out loud, asking others to read it for me, until eventually most of the yellow was gone. I could point to some of the pioneering work of Translation Studies: to Jean-Paul Vinay and Jean Darbelnet's essay, first published in the 1950s, which breaks down the most common strategies of translation into seven basic procedures, a 'methodology for translation'. Among them is the procedure they call 'modulation', which involves moving from a general verb to one that it is more specific, as I did with my translation of *faire* (a verb which can mean a great deal of things, covering a large semantic territory, that I translated locally and more narrowly as *to write*). I could direct you to Antoine Berman's work in the 1980s, specifically to an essay translated by Laurence Venuti offering his analytic of translation, which shows how these broad strategies are also, always, and in their own way distortive. I could point you to Susan Bernofsky's much more recent illuminating essay on her own translation process, full of local detail about working from the German into English, which I have referred students to so many times in my teaching, sharing out its insights and commonly deployable working methods. Or indeed to Jacqueline Guillemin-Flescher's *Syntaxe comparée du français et de l'anglais: problèmes de traduction,* whose case study is *Madame Bovary*. But even these textured descriptions of the translation process, their breakdowns of the different strategies that translators employ, however real and pertinent they may be, and however common to all translational activity everywhere, operate – they necessarily operate – on a level of abstraction from the living life of translating *this work in particular* which, because it involves life, and people, because it involves a relation between this culture and that one, this writing subject and that one, as well as reading and feeling and mistakes, because it involves making a risky decision about *every single local element* of the writing written in *this* language, because it involves taking responsibility, in this way, for *every single one of its details* as I set about writing the whole again in *this* language and circumstance, is each time different.

WHO REFUSES TO LET GO OF HER TRANSLATIONS UNTIL SHE FEELS SHE HAS WRITTEN THE BOOKS HERSELF (OR, TRANSLATION AND THE PRINCIPLE OF TACT)

In his book on the English-language translations and translators of Thomas Mann, David Horton shares a detail from a translation conference held in Vancouver in 2002 (a scene he finds first described in an essay on literary translation by Lew Zybatow). How, when the Norwegian translation scholar Per Qvale quoted, to the room, the line about Helen Lowe-Porter 'never dispatching a translation unless she had the feeling she had done it herself', everybody laughed.

There was, apparently, 'a general outburst of mirth'.

'Each time that in my pleasure, my desire, or my distress, the other's discourse (often well-meaning, innocent) reduces me to a case that fits an all-purpose explanation or classification in the most normal way, I feel that there is a breach of the principle of tact,' says Barthes in *The Neutral*, the notes for the middle lecture course translated by Rosalind Krauss and Denis Hollier. The principle of tact: understood here as an attentiveness to difference, an effort made to not treat all things in the same way; 'active protests' or 'unexpected parryings' against the all-purpose explanation.

Everybody laughed. Which suggests that operative in the conference room there must have been some general, already established understanding of how a translator *should* feel about her work: a better, more considered, less laughable kind of feeling.

On the one hand, I am outraged that Lowe-Porter's position should have been laughed at: on the lived-out level of writing, the setting down of language, the making of a new volume of words on the basis of an existing one, she *did* write the books herself. Of course she did. How could anyone maintain otherwise? On the other, I can see, of course, that it is complicated. Perhaps it was funny because it is complicated; perhaps the room was filled with uncertain, nervous laughter: because while it seems clear that the conception and the first execution – in other words, the authorship – of *The Magic Mountain* belongs to Thomas Mann (she didn't write the novel, she would have been incapable of writing it, as Lowe-Porter would no doubt have also been very ready to concede), still a doubt remains: What to do with – how exactly are we to think about – the labour of translation if it *doesn't* on some level entail doing it herself? Or indeed with the status of the object that her labour produces?

The scholar and theorist Emily Apter has published some fascinating discussions of the ways in which translation can make authorial ownership nervous. How, as she writes, 'translation offers a particularly rich focus for discussions of creative property and the limits of ownership because it is a peculiar genre ... in what is perhaps a unique case of art as authorized plagiarism or legal appropriationism, the translation is encouraged to pilfer the original with no risk of copyright infringement or allegations of forgery. It is granted this license because it implicitly claims to be of the original, that is to say, possessed of no autonomous textual identity. Translation thus challenges legalistic norms of ownable intellectual property ... [throwing] into arrears the whole idea that authors of "originals" are the sole owners of their literary property.' It seems to me that the worry – the nervous laughter – stems from the translation's claim to be *of the original*, and thereby – Apter's 'that is to say' – 'possessed of no autonomous textual identity'. I would suggest that this claim gets made more explicitly than 'implicitly': by announcing itself to be a translation, a translation clearly states its derivativeness, pointing to the original as the condition of its coming into being, and perhaps it is this, this assertion of having sprung from, of being *of* and therefore still belonging to the original (if only in the sense that it can always be checked and measured against it), that makes me feel confident in my reading. Assertive in my sense that when it comes to *The Magic Mountain* – without any German, without, as yet, any prospect of reading the novel in German: Yes, I too have read it. But must it follow from this that the book I have read, that I am still repeatedly reading – my copy of *The Magic Mountain*, with its bashed-up cover – has 'no autonomous textual identity'? Which would be, as Apter points out, its legal status, the basis upon which the translator was enabled to write something wholly derived without risking infringement?

Yes and no, it seems, depending on the pressure you want to put on the word 'autonomous'.

'Think of a kitchen table ... when you're not there,' advised Andrew. He meant this as a way for Lily to ponder the degree to which objects can be said to exist independently of a person being there to observe them – a proposition that Lily finds quite difficult to think. But it reminds me, oddly, of those author photos that are sometimes published in the book pages of the newspaper: the successful and much-translated author sitting at her writing desk; displayed on the shelves behind her are all the different language editions of her best-selling book. The French translation, the German, the Japanese, the Norwegian... All these further books derived from the same single source, now lined up the one alongside the other on her shelves. All these further books that are in some sense – some legal sense, but also, perhaps, in some experiential sense, if one could find and check with a reader capable of reading them all – *more or less* identifiably the same book. Lined up together on the shelves like this, the same book written again and again in the many languages I am unable to read, published in contexts so distant from, for example, the cosy comfort of the writer's London study, or indeed of my own living room, as I read the book pages online at home, the translations appear virtual, sort of propositional – that is, fictional: like so many alternative fictions of the original – not, in and of themselves, altogether real.

But they are, of course: each one is (also) a whole book made, written. Each one is a book now acting on its own terms in the world; a thing currently being bought and sold and read and held and dropped and lived with and discussed. Looking at the photograph of the author's shelves, I feel like I should know this, but thinking it – *really thinking* about all these different relations produced by and now existing independently of whatever the original context of writing might have been – requires a further and concerted effort of the imagination.

'Think of a kitchen table ... when you're not there'. In *To the Lighthouse*, Lily does, indeed, think of it. She often thinks of and pictures a table, 'a scrubbed kitchen table' – but she is there, too. Making her way through the garden and down to the beach: 'It lodged now in the fork of a pear tree, for they had reached the orchard ... And with a painful effort of concentration, she focused her mind, not upon the silver-bossed bark of the tree, or upon its fish-shaped leaves, but upon a phantom kitchen table, one of those scrubbed board tables, grained and knotted whose virtue seems to be laid bare by years of muscular integrity, which stuck there, its four legs in the air.' To see a table, to actually see a kitchen table – not as an example or an abstraction, not as an object existing independently of anyone there to observe or work at or eat at it, uninscribed in anyone's actual living life – but as scrubbed and grained and knotted. It is easy not to think about kitchen tables. In the same way, holding to my analogy, as it is easy not to think about translation. To do so, to make translation appear as a once-made (a twice-made) whole, a durable and integral and yet un-independent, never quite *autonomous* whole, takes a painful effort of concentration. It requires something like an effort of defamiliarization – of the order, perhaps, of imagining a kitchen table upside down, lodged now in the fork of a pear tree, its four legs in the air.

When the translator's sense of her own working process was communicated to the room, everybody laughed. There was, apparently, 'a general outburst of mirth'.

Can I tell you that when people talk to me about what I do, even when they solicit me to do what I do (to come along and translate a conference paper, someone's article or someone's book), I sometimes, often, feel like I am being pressed up against some pre-established agreement of what the work involves, some already decided general sense of how I must think about it and how I must feel? Pressed up against or pressed in by what I realize is a wholly normal, widespread and well-intentioned understanding of the practice of translation. As – what? As generous, typically. As selfless (involving setting my own self, my fascinations and feelings aside). As in-service to the world. Where my service is understood to be a process of conversion, a sort of universal procedure, empty of content. A process abstractable from the materials it is working on, the contexts it is working in, and the bodies of those engaged with it. An all-purpose process that can be set to work and made to fit all occasions because translation is more or less translation everywhere.

An understanding that's not wrong.

Not at all wrong.

For the fact is, if we are able to point to and talk about translation as we do it or we see it – as it appears and operates in all contexts and directions all the time – it is because these occurrences do indeed have something in common. It is because we have witnessed, or more likely have been told, that the action of changing words from one language into another has occurred, which is the way the dictionary describes it. That, at least, is its first definition (the second proposes the more general *conversion from one form or medium to another*, in recognition of all the many other ways we use the term). It is because there must indeed be continuity, a commonality, a minimal set of gestures shared between the act of translating Barthes's lecture notes from French into English, for example, and the act of doing apparently the same but into German this time, or Italian, or live translating them out loud, or tapping them into Google Translate to see what the algorithm throws up, or translating the work of another French writer into English, or working from English into French this time, or trying to make a start with Dutch.

I might confess to feeling pressed in by it, but this general working definition is not wrong.

And nor, as it turns out, is it too narrow, or too small.

What Barthes identifies as a breach of tact is the feeling of being reduced to a category that is too big. A great big class of actors and of activity, a kind of catch-all box. One that holds us all – translation is more or less translation, and translators are more or less translators, everywhere – but for just that reason cannot begin to attend to our different motivations, our specific desires, our peculiar joys and distresses.

'When I receive one of Dr Mann's works to translate, what I try to do is read it, not merely to get the sense but the flavour, the mood and tempo, the atmosphere,' writes Lowe-Porter in the long letter her daughters quoted. 'Well, then I try to decide whether the book has its peculiar characteristics of style which it would be my duty to represent ... And when I got this well into my ear and feeling, I would use it to clothe as meticulous, supple and intuitive a rendering of the original as I possibly could ... It is clear that the author of *Buddenbrooks*, *Der Zauberberg*, the Joseph series, and *Lotte* would and did fuse his matter and style into an organic whole. The translations ought to show an effort on the part of the translator to do the same.'

Clearly, observes David Horton, 'Lowe-Porter felt empowered to intervene in the originals as long as the aesthetic qualities she perceived in the source-language work were reconstituted' in the target-language text. But the 'extent to which [she] was in fact aware of Mann's "larger creative purposes" is open to question.' He notes how apologetic and self-deprecating her translator's notes could be; how in her letters she worried over her 'inadequacy as a linguist, as a speaker of German, as a poet.' And yet, how she remained 'fundamentally convinced of her qualities and qualifications as the mediator of Thomas Mann.' Her interventions were extensive (in the form of 'reformulations and transpositions, omissions and additions', all the mistakes that Buck lists). But as both Theo Hermans, in his separate discussion of the *TLS* controversy, and Horton point out, it was Lowe-Porter's explicit project to make a translation that would work well in English; to render Mann's prose in such a way that the books would be readable and on that basis desirable in the new market. And they were: again, her translations were both well-received and commercially successful. Horton concedes that by our current standards, 'the line between empathetic identification, idiosyncratic assimilation and problematic appropriation' in her approach can seem 'truly thin'. Yet, as Horton also shows, her practice of extensively excising and adding (in keeping with her own vision of the whole and her concern for her English-speaking readership) was common among her contemporaries. Which is precisely the point that Venuti makes in his letter to the *TLS*: standards for what makes a good translation, for what the work of translation involves, and for how the translator should think and feel are historically and culturally determined and – they change. In *Thomas Mann in English*, David Horton takes this seriously. With its detailed discussions of the specific context in which Lowe-Porter was translating, its effort to research and understand her particular approach to her work and the pressures that were put upon her, in its refusal to laugh a bit more at her position and the translations she spent over twenty years of her lifetime writing, considering them instead as carefully written whole but un-autonomous things, written herself but not altogether *by* herself (in solitude, perhaps, but never exactly alone), Horton's book reads to me like an exercise in tact.

The word Barthes uses in French is *délicatesse* – a beautiful sequence of syllables to walk through the mouth. A decisive principle of the oeuvre, writes Tiphaine Samoyault, *délicatesse* is 'the contrary of arrogance' and another name for what Barthes called 'the neutral'. But where the neutral is imagined as a utopia (in grammar, the neutral or neuter is neither masculine nor feminine, neither active nor passive; in politics, Barthes sees it as a refusal to take sides on complex conflictual questions phrased in such a way as to permit only yes/no answers), *délicatesse* is the name given to the small-scale, everyday practice of values such as goodwill and attentiveness, what Barthes also calls 'sweetness' (*la douceur*), values in the form of behaviours that parry the already decided, the apparent self-evidence, the all-purpose explanation – and attend instead to those small, fleeting and fragile moments in life where, as Samoyault puts it, 'individualities truly express themselves in their truth.'

Tact is a brilliant translation by Krauss and Hollier, I think. The same short ah, the hard c and the t; the implication of handling, touching. More agile – nimbler – than 'consideration', say, or 'thoughtfulness'; not quite as strategic or as calculating as 'diplomacy'; more robust (healthier?) than its cognate, 'delicacy'.

Although of course their word-choice gains in specificity by way of its relations to these other, presumably considered and rejected possibilities.

I say 'of course', but I don't think I fully grasped Ferdinand de Saussure's early twentieth-century insight into the way words (or what he calls linguistic signs) work. How, as he puts it in the *Course in General Linguistics* (which I read in Roy Harris's translation), they acquire their meanings relationally within what appears to be a closed system, until I started translating. Signs are like chess pieces, I remember reading. Where, say, for example: the rook is missing, and it's probably down the back of the sofa somewhere or maybe not. But, don't worry; it doesn't matter; we can still play anyway, we can use a coin or a piece of Lego or something else instead. And together we'll observe how the substitute acquires the meaning and the function of a rook, how it starts behaving as a rook, not because of its now-emerging rook-like qualities, but because of the way it takes its place within the system of the board: through *not being* a queen, a knight, a bishop, or a pawn.

Or, words less like objects now, with a bit more heat and air: the two of us trying to get comfortable on a blow-up mattress, and this shared awareness that if I roll over too heavily over *here* it will push up a part of you over *there*.

The point being that when a translator chooses *this* over *that* it is not only because of what *this* is and does, the particular history of the word, its sedimented etymology, but also because of it *not* being or doing *this* or *that* within the range of possibilities offered to her in her own language, each one of them determining – lifting, depressing, wobbling – the other. It is this awareness of what is always the *unbounded* whole, the loosely demarcated bed of the translation she is making, both as a volume in and of itself and as it opens out relationally onto and is written into the language and culture of the translation more generally (what Venuti terms a process of 'domestic inscription') that will inform how each one of her local decisions get made and how, in the best-case scenario, they will come to feel necessary. Sometimes, often, because *that* will be needed later. To serve, maybe, as the translation for the second term in a comparison that the translator knows will be made pages ahead, for example when Barthes talks of *discretion* (pointing to the roots it shares with 'to discern', 'to differentiate', 'to separate out') as a further manifestation of tact, or of politeness being to one side of both (too codified, too inflexible). Sometimes, often, because of an awareness – insofar as it is possible to be fully aware, within the limits of her reading time, her lifetime – of all the other phrases and word-choices that the text-to-be-translated is speaking to, or might come, eventually, to speak to.

Here is a verb, and it appears to be one that I know well; a verb like *faire*. I have seen it translated elsewhere, so many times, in these common-sensical, wholly appropriate ways. Yes, but (the translator asks herself – some years after the fact is still asking herself): What if *in this case* the case were different?

Tact: the art of not treating all things in the same way. Of treating *what appears to be the same* as though different. 'A fine responsiveness to the concrete,' as philosopher Martha Nussbaum defines it in her readings of Henry James; that is, 'the ability to discern, acutely and responsively, the salient features of one's particular situation.' For example, notes Barthes: Do not (you wouldn't) attack an antique with the zeal of a Dutch housewife (would you?). All those eighteenth-century paintings I think Barthes must have had in mind: the smiling maids, creamy forearms and thick fingers, scouring at whatever comes to hand.

'A little art,' Helen Lowe-Porter called it. The writing of translations: this little art. I accept her *little* for as long as I can oppose it to trivial, to minor, to young. To the extent that I can hear it – that I can make it – speak of an art of attending to all the small differences. The example Barthes offers, as a counter to the Dutch housewife, comes from *The Book of Tea* by Okakura Kakuzō, the chapter on flowers: the ancient art of floriculture. In the Tang and Sung dynasties, Barthes part-quotes, 'a special attendant was detailed to wait upon each flower and to wash its leaves with soft brushes made of rabbit hair. It has been written that the peony should be bathed by a handsome maiden in full costume, that a winter plum should be watered by a pale, slender monk.'

To each flower its own special attendant.

Le cours, c'est comme une fleur, noted Barthes. A lecture course is like a flower – a note provisonally written down only ever to be spoken aloud. In the sense that its life-span is short. That it belongs to the share of a life's work that is ephemeral. In the sense that it will, it must – the verb Barthes uses is *passer*. A word left to shimmer at the end of the sentence, whose meaning is not yet altogether determined by the syntax, nor indeed by the object of the sentence. Still caught up in my long effort to translate this line, I look up *passer* in the French dictionary. I find, among all the many definitions: 'to be animated by a movement'; 'to visit for a short time with no intention of staying'; 'to traverse a substance, a material, a place'; 'to leave one place to go to another'; 'to change state, or status'; '(in relation to time) to go by'; 'to disappear, to cease being'. Towards the very bottom of the list I find: to lose colour, in the way a fabric can fade, bleaching out from having been left too long in the sun.

In the account I'm offering, the translator adjusts her manner of handling, the form of her care, in response to what is being held (to each flower its own attendant).

But – it is worth stressing again – this is not to say that her efforts will keep her from doing harm, or giving offence.

She may fail to recognize the winter plum, and treat it as something else.

She may recognize the plum for what it is and what it needs but can do nothing to change the fact that she is not the pale, slender monk capable of addressing it properly. Dorothy Bussy to Gide, in a letter dated 11 May 1946: 'And now I am going to say something very serious. I realise at last that I have been one of the great disappointments of your life. You would have liked (for sentimental not rational reasons) to be translated into English by a young man – especially *Les Nourritures*, especially *Si le Grain ne meurt*, especially *Thésée*.' Gide had written of his preference for what he called a 'deep-voiced' translator. Then, in the next paragraph: 'How can you, who pride yourself particularly in imitating a woman's, a young girl's voice, think that the opposite impersonation is impossible?'.

Is that right? It is such a powerful, pervasive idea: that out ahead, on the horizon of approaching history there is, there will be, coming, the *right* translator, the one always meant to be more congruously paired with this writer, this work, who will, this time, once and for all, handle it appropriately. It is the thought – or the hope – animating the review that says: this is disappointing, this unlikely match; this one is regrettable. This one, as David Luke maintained, writing to the *TLS* in support of Timothy Buck's devastating review, is 'debased' and 'a continuing scandal'.

But no. I don't think so. Books don't come with designated translators; they don't have built-in protocols, accepted codes of behaviour which can be followed (success) or ignored (failure). Our manners of translating have to be each time improvised and invented in new response to the book in hand. Like meeting someone late at night at a party. Then bumping into them again the morning after and taking measure of the small charge in the air between the two of us; registering, in all the little ways, how things were last night, how different they might be today. Tact, Barthes tells us, requires the punctilious elimination of repetition: tact is *scared*, it is hurt by repetition. And so, as a principle, it is, in principle, unexpected and so un-systematizable, unparadigmatizable. This time a slender monk with his soft-haired brush, the next a plumper one, and the time after that – why not? – a handsome middle-class maiden in full costume.

'Dear and beloved, it is so sweet for me to think that I know you so well and so secretly,' wrote Bussy to Gide in a letter dated 1 October 1930: 'Nobody could possibly imagine our incongruous friendship.'

Yes, but. Hold on: with this principle of tact, is Barthes not speaking very generally, is he not in the process of devising some new all-purpose classification for a behaviour, for a manner of being, that he is also saying is not generalizable and, more precisely, would *fail*, if it were codifiable, predictable? Yes, says Barthes. You're right, in a telegrammatic note which, in Krauss and Hollier's translation, reads: 'I did it because there is a residue: residue = nothing more to say than the fact itself: that which one can posit, state, say, tell: we enter the discourse of anecdote.' We can offset the rush to the general with the slower, finer phrasing of the facts themselves, possibly; with 'the salient features of one's particular situation'. Let me tell you something that happened to me. Let me tell you a little bit about how things are, how they have been, for me. A table by the window; boys leaping, sometimes, from wall-top to wall-top outside. A book on the table that was never meant to be a book. Notes for a sequence of lectures that were intended to be delivered – to pass, to go by, and then fade: *Le cours c'est comme une fleur, vous permettez, mais qui va passer*. A lecture course is what *will* pass, it is what *will* fade, notes Barthes. But of course it didn't: the project of translation was to make another book, a further book on the basis of what was never written to become a book. In the translation of this preoccupying sentence, there are norms and codes that apply – general behaviours that might work for this situation, and that I could use again elsewhere, or teach. There's also something unrepeatable.

'I am to see Madame Knopf this afternoon at 4,' wrote Gide on 18 November 1929. He and Bussy shared an American publisher with Thomas Mann, but whereas the Knopfs worked hard to secure Lowe-Porter's position as Mann's translator, with Bussy it was different. 'Tea is enough,' Gide went on, 'I shrank from the prospect of dinner. I dare her to prove to me that your translations are bad; the various reviews of you I receive from America are on the contrary so laudatory of you that I doubt she will risk a fresh attack.' In a footnote, editor Richard Tedeschi narrates how, from the beginning, 'the Knopf company and its agents had maintained that D. B.'s translations were poor, and had encouraged Gide to entrust his work to other translators.'

Following that early miserable translation class, my first self-directed effort at French to English translating was the first chapter of Gide's *Les Faux-Monnayeurs* (1925). The book had been set reading on a course I took in my last undergraduate year; I knew very little about Paris, was learning a bit about French culture, and this is impossible, I remember thinking: the particular location of the jardin du Luxembourg, where it is and what it means; the fontaine Médicis where the young lycéens would gather to talk *art, philosophie, sports, politique et littérature*; what their kind of lycée was, in Paris's fifth arrondissement, what it meant and what it still means; the way they wouldn't talk, actually, they *causaient* – they would chat, or something like it; the way so much of this opening section unfolds in the curious ongoing repeated everyday action of the *imparfait*; the way they'd shake each other's hands just like that, casually; an everyday greeting among adolescent boys which struck me, then, still close enough to my own teenage years, as wholly unimaginable; the way one of the boys sits on a bench, reading *Action française* – a wooden bench painted dark green, probably, contrasting with movable metal chairs that now also furnish the jardin du Luxembourg, their distinctive – beautiful, I think – soft pale green, how cold they can be (when were the metal chairs introduced I wonder? What is the precise cultural significance of the *Action française*? I'd have to find out); the way Lucien, who writes poetry, is shy, but will venture to tell a distracted Olivier about his project for a novel nevertheless: what I would like, he says, is to tell a story, not from the point of view of a character, but of a place – *tiens*, he says, familiarly, because he is confiding in his friend – *tiens, par exemple*, a place like this one; it would be the story of an *allée de jardin*, like this one, and would narrate what happens there, or here (*ce qui s'y passe*:

what goes on, what goes by, what passes, perhaps, gaining and slowly losing its lustre, its colour fading out) from morning till night. The way Gide's sentences unfold at the rhythm of a young man thinking, precise clauses held together so delicately by just a comma; the use of repetition, of idiom: *Il y viendrait d'abord des bonnes d'enfants, des nourrices, avec des rubans... Non, non... d'abord des gens tout gris, sans sexe ni âge, pour balayer l'allée, arroser l'herbe, changer les fleurs, enfin la scène et le décor avant l'ouverture des grilles, tu comprends?* What to do with this, how possibly to render all this?

But then I began; I think I must have begun, amateur-ishly. The project of it – at once contained, constrained, and open to me. Open, as well, to the future, since it's all to come: nothing has yet been decided. With translation, you begin: at the risk of getting it all wrong and with the original pages next to you as you write (to go back to, to keep repeatedly going back to), you set out, you begin to test out possible solutions to the questions and problems that the project of translating (translating, setting down language, using and working its materials) causes to emerge, and something happens. Some new thing starts to get made in the frame of againness; something that is *of the original*, yes, but that will extend beyond the reach of it, the purview of it, since it is being made by someone else, by me now, and will be read, perhaps, by some or many others, all of them to come and for the moment elsewhere. Dorothy Bussy's translation, *The Counterfeiters*, was published in 1931 (the American edition was retitled *The Coiners* – a decision made by her publishers that in her letters she calls 'a sore point in [her] professional career'). The jardin du Luxembourg is translated as 'The Luxembourg Gardens' – an indication of how accepted standards for translation practice change (a translator would be likely to retain the French appellation now); there is a note explaining the term *bachot* ('schoolboy's slang for the baccalauréat examination'), which Bernard had stayed at home to cram for, reminding us, here on the very first page of the novel, even as we receive it in English, that everything is to be imagined as if it were narrated in French; the *allées* of the park (is it a park or are they formal gardens?) are paths. Reading the translation against the original I could enumerate all the further differences. Look, here is difference, I could say, and look! Look! Here is more difference – and this, too, could have been done differently (as every translation could). Meanwhile,

"'What I should like,'" said Lucien,

in Bussy's 1931 translation,

"'would be to tell the story – no, not of a person, but of a place – well, for instance, of a garden path, like this – just tell what happens in it from morning to evening. First of all, come the children's nurses and the children, and the babies' nurses with ribbons in their caps ... No, no, ... first of all, people who are grey all over and ageless and sexless and who come to sweep the path, and water the grass, and change the flowers – in fact, to set the stage and get ready the scenery before the opening of the gates. D'you see?'"

Barthes lived very close to those gates, of course. Walking up to the jardin du Luxembourg from the rue Servandoni he would have come into the park on the side of the shady fountain, the place where the boys meet and chat. I think again of the woman he describes glimpsed from his window in the lecture notes on *How to Live Together*: the mother (or was it one of those nurses or nannies? – there are still so many of them working in the jardin du Luxembourg) walking with her child, with her charge, in all likelihood on their way to or home from the park, pushing the empty buggy out in front of her, while holding the little boy by the hand, while walking at her own pace, too fast for the small boy. The woman – in his editor's introduction, Claude Coste calls her 'the bad mother' – seen to be keeping, implacably, to her own walking rhythm, not noticing that she's dragging the child along, seemingly unaware that she is forcing him to run to keep up. 'And she's his mother!' Barthes assumes and exclaims. An image briefly described, but one that Barthes insists is central – crystallizing – for all that he would come to think and say about rhythm and power, about the effects of imposing one rhythm on – overwriting – another.

A translation should be redone every twenty-five years. It's something I often hear people say – it is something that Barthes says in his lectures on the haiku. And I'm sure he's right: standards change, languages change, our manner of doing things, our interests and our energies change. In a chapter on the English-language translations of Barthes's work published in the early 1980s, Elisabeth W. Bruss shows how the timings of those translations imposed a new rhythm of reading and reception. How translation, with its necessary lags, its inevitable out-of-sync-ness, enacts exactly the kind of rhythmic incompatibility that Barthes observes from his window – arguably all the time. The first two translations to appear were 'Criticism as Language' in 1963, commissioned for publication in English, and *On Racine*, translated by Richard Howard in 1964, coming just a year after its publication in French.

Then there was a gap of three years.

Then, a second flurry of translation: this phase, says Bruss, 'stretched roughly between 1967 (which saw the British appearance of the combined edition of *Writing Degree Zero* and *Elements of Semiology* co-translated by Annette Lavers and Colin Smith – books that in French had been published a decade apart) and 1972 (when the American edition of *Critical Essays* appeared in Howard's translation, along with the joint Anglo-American publication of Annette Lavers's selections from *Mythologies*)'.

Another gap.

Then, from 1975 on, 'another series of translations was issued in America and the UK at the rate of one or two a year': *S/Z,* translated by Richard Miller in 1975 (it had appeared in French five years earlier), *Image/Music/Text,* translated by Stephen Heath in 1977, and the last sequence of books: *Roland Barthes by Roland Barthes* in 1977

341

and *A Lover's Discourse* in 1978, *Camera Lucida* in 1980, all in Richard Howard's translations.

These timings, as Bruss shows on a chart comparing the sequence of publishing in France to the UK and America, had far more to do with the rise and fall of our Anglo-American interests than Barthes's 'own productive rhythms'. But they were not without their effects (the imposition of one rhythm on another, as notes Barthes in reference to the walking woman, so profoundly out of step with her charge, is never without its effects). They served to produce new relationships between the works, enabling those first written further apart to be read together, and those originally written the one after the other to be read much further apart. The outcome of this redistribution, Bruss argues, 'was to define Barthes's structuralist writings as the core of all that came before and after them'. To create a neat three-part narrative – beginning; high structuralist middle; late, personal, fragmented, novelistic end – which then formed the basis of a whole variety of different and competing stories about Barthes's development as a writer, theorist and critic.

There were some commentators, for example, who saw this arc as the tale of 'an upstart intruder' declining into 'an aging and outmoded writer'.

Or '(in another version) a writer who grew embarrassed and unsure and in the late works began to betray his own best work'.

Or '(in another version still)' a writer who matured 'to the point where he could finally disdain the changing whims of fashion and write solely for himself'.

The translations – the approaches of the individual translators, their local decisions – clearly played their part in this, too. As Bruss describes, different translators saw and valued different aspects of Barthes's work, and she reads 'what each took to be essential to Barthes's prose – the conceptual machinery, the social subversions, or the cadences' as a clue to their own preferred story. She considers, for example, Stephen Heath's Barthes: 'a deliberately "difficult" writer' in *Image/Music/Text* 'whose language is kept from merging too easily with entrenched, and idiomatic, English.' And compares with the 'fluidity and grace' of Howard's translations of the later works; a change in translator and in manner which would reinforce the impression – not entirely mistaken – of the late 'emergence of a more accessible, more "readable" Barthes'.

The recent English-language translations of Barthes's lecture and seminar notes in 2005, 2011 and 2013, together with the posthumously published *Mourning Diary*, which appeared in Richard Howard's translation in 2010, a new translation of *Incidents* by Teresa Lavender Fagan the same year, and the five volumes of essays and interviews currently appearing in translations by Chris Turner, could be said to form a fourth wave of translation activity, making a different gathering of apparently new works, and writing a further chapter in the story of Barthes's work in English. What is this doing to our sense of his work? The lectures that feel only recently published were of course originally produced – drafted and publicly delivered, with no view to publication – contemporaneously with the books published in the late 1970s. For me, in the translations I claim to have written myself, my preference has been for warmth. For the warmth I feel in Barthes's mode of address. Its reach: the way it seemed to include me. And, in amongst its admissions of grief, the sharp pain of recent loss, the phrasing and pushing at the vital questions – 'How does one organize one's sense of being in the world?' is how Lucy O'Meara so beautifully summarizes them; and then, 'How could the negative aspects of that world be imagined otherwise?' – its humour (there are jokes in the lectures: really, quite a number of jokes).

By Barthes's every-twenty-five years calculation, it is now time for some of the books to be translated again.

Will they be, I wonder? And what might this do to our sense of the books, to the teaching notes, to the stories we'll tell about the relations between them, to our understanding of the body of work as a whole?

What would it be like, for instance, to read a book called *The Light Room* (maybe? why not? Perhaps there is a reason why, but I have never really been able to think why not). A book this time subtitled: *Note on Photography*. And to read it now, having read the lectures, and so not as an ending, no longer as *the ultimate last work*, which is how I have so often read it described, but as part of a future-orientated interest in the practice of notation, of which photography would be just one particular instance among others (ideas that Barthes works out in one of the lectures); in other words, to think of that book as part of the inquiry into how to pass from the shortest form, the smallest note, to the long form, how to make something more extended and stretched and continuous out of these intense capturings, these slivers of lived experience; to think of that book as having been written somewhere on the path towards the novel-to-come.

And what would it be like, I wonder, to read – to newly reread – *Roland Barthes*? Or a book this time titled *Fragments of a lover's* (of a loving?) *discourse*?

The love letter is 'a special dialectic'; at once coded and expressive. 'Charged', as Barthes writes in *A Lover's Discourse*, 'with the longing to signify desire'.

One special feature of the Gide-Bussy correspondence is its bilingualism: with very few exceptions, across so many years of writing to each other, Bussy would write to Gide in English, and Gide would reply in French. Hence Gide's request in a very early letter: '*Allow me to write in French, because* I have precise things to tell you and am afraid of not being clear enough.' But, as the citation shows, the bilingualism wasn't preserved in the English translation (how could it have been?). Here the italics do the work of indicating when Gide was *really* writing in English. They ask us to imagine it. In his introduction to the French edition, Jean Lambert expresses regret that Bussy's letters could not be presented in their original form. But he's also intrigued as to why Bussy should have kept choosing to write in English in the first place. Unlike Gide, her competence in her second language, he notes, was exemplary. What's more, the correspondence was to go on for more than thirty years, so it can't just have been a matter of continuing her role as Gide's English instructor. Perhaps it had to do, Lambert suggests, with a similar feeling of ease in her own language, and her own concern for precision. Lambert picks up especially on the way Bussy alternately exploits and gets exasperated by the English distinction between 'to like' and 'to love' (*aimer* in French) in her letters. To the point where one day she decides all of a sudden to write:

Je vous aime, cela sonne mieux en français.

I love you, it sounds better in French (would be the obvious – the only? – translation).

But the *vous*.

It is striking and important: what it is to make a declaration of love with a formal 'you'.

I can't render it in English.

Or I can, I could, but not in the same number of words, and not with the same economy of expression: I'd need time, and space, a whole book of notes, rising to the top of the page, possibly, in order to unfold and explain, exhaustively, all the connotations and denotations of this small compaction of language.

In other words: I could write something for you on this moment, of this moment, but I'm not sure I'd call it a translation.

There is a powerful irony in the fact that two accomplished writer-translators chose to solve the problem of all the subtle differences between their respective languages and cultures by refusing to translate. And yet, that decision is what makes something of the stakes involved in translating appear:

'My dear Friend,' Bussy writes to Gide on 5 November 1918. 'Do you know that this beginning to a letter which is such an ordinary one in French is very unusual in English?'

'But a nice one all the same and I like it.'

She signs off: 'Ever yours –

do you know that this ending to a letter which would sound so terrific in French is very common in English and just implies a pleasant friendly intimacy?'

Some ten years later, on 19 November 1927, Gide hazards a letter in English. He ends it: 'But forever yours, André Gide.'

'Your English is very good,' writes Bussy in reply.

'Only a slight nuance may be pointed out. Though you may sign "Ever yours" to anybody you know fairly well without compromising yourself in the least, "forever yours" is practically equal to a declaration!

I am afraid I can't give you the credit of knowing this.

But I – fully aware, call myself: Forever yours, D. B.'

Throughout the correspondence, Bussy alternately delights in or agonizes over the small disjunctions between the codes of letter-writing in English and French, appraising the degrees of intimacy and feeling, measuring what these stock phrases usually mean against what – when transposed into another language, or when newly used by someone writing in English as their second language – they might be made to mean. The effect is cumulative: Bussy's comments on such forms of address were a way, I think, for her to keep more or less indirectly expressing her love for Gide; at the same time, they make for this wholly compelling account of a lived – never resolved, ongoing, mobile and always intensely charged, always intensely *accompanied* – translating experience.

For me, the most powerful moment in that account occurs towards the very end. Gide and Bussy are old now. 'Dear Gide. It is no use telling you that I am growing very old now ... that my hair and teeth are falling out, my eyes, my ears, my memory failing, that I hardly dare walk without a stick, that perhaps you wouldn't recognize me' (it is October 1944; she was seventy-nine). 'But! I prefer to think of you...' The epilogue to the *Selected Letters* reproduces a page written by Roger Martin du Gard on his sense of the relation between Bussy and Gide (Martin du Gard was a friend of them both, and the French translator of Bussy's novel *Olivia*). He writes: 'I who have heard [Gide's] confidences concerning Dorothy since 1920 and in the following years, I remember with no possible error that he never felt for her more than a compassionate and deeply tender friendship...' He didn't love her as she loved him, clearly. But he wrote this: 'You cannot imagine, my dear, what attraction I feel for her face, and always more so, truly, with the years ... Yes. I find the expression of that face exquisite ... I look at her now with more emotion than ever.'

In a letter dated 22 August 1948, Gide writes to Bussy of his own failing health. They are aged eighty-four and eighty-three – growing very old now. He remarks on two different questions of translation: whether Bussy would undertake to translate his *Feuillets d'automne* and the Martin du Gard translation of Bussy's novel in progress, whose merit Gide had finally recognized in a recent telegram (referencing Gide's early reactions to the first volume of *In Search of Lost Time*, which were famously dismissive, it read: 'As repentant and embarrassed as with Proust, Gide'). As usual, Gide's letter is written in French. But it concludes with a sentence that shifts suddenly from French into English – as far as I can tell, for the first time since the mistake over 'forever yours' some twenty years earlier. The sentence reads:

'*De tout mon cœur bien fatigué*, I love you.'

(With all my tired heart, I love you).

'Like desire, the love letter waits for an answer; it implicitly enjoins the other to reply...' writes Barthes.

And then, on *'Je-t'-aime'*/'I-love-you': 'Everything is in the speaking of it: it is a "formula," but this formula corresponds to no ritual; the situations in which I say *I-love-you* cannot be classified: *I-love-you* is irrepressible and unforeseeable.'

Bussy's reply to Gide is dated six days later.

She begins the letter with some words on Gide's health, she accepts the commission to translate the *Feuillets d'automne*; she writes of the two books the whole of London was talking about (*The Trials of Oscar Wilde*, and Graham Greene's *The Heart of the Matter*), her correspondence with Roger Martin du Gard.

The letter is relatively long.

It is only at the very end that she addresses what Gide had written. She writes:

'I hope all this stuff won't bore and tire you. Dear Gide, at any rate it won't make your heart beat as one sentence in your letter made mine beat this morning.

But then I say to myself, "He doesn't know English well enough to quite realize what he was saying!" Oh dear! What nonsense from your friend aged 83 last birthday... D. B.'

So her letter ends.

In the preface to his *Critical Essays*, Barthes describes writing a letter to a friend who had just lost a loved one, wanting to express his sympathy. But finding it difficult. Feeling that all the words at his disposal are unsatisfactory: they are merely 'phrases', and do nothing to convey what he feels. He goes on, in Richard Howard's translation: 'I ... realize that the message I want to send to this friend, which is my sympathy itself, could be reduced to a single word: "condolences". Yet the very purpose of the communication is opposed to this, for the message would be cold and consequently reversed, when what I want to communicate is precisely the warmth of my sympathy. I conclude that in order to correct my message (that is, in order for it to be exact), I must not only vary it but that this variation must be original and seemingly invented.' The demand to come up with a new, unexpected – some unforeseen – variation, in light of these new circumstances, taking a measure of how things are – this demand, wrote Barthes, is the demand of literature. This is 'its precious indirection'. Indeed, 'it is only by submitting to its law that I may communicate what I mean with exactitude; in literature as in private communication, to be least "false" I must be most "original", or if you prefer, indirect.' With his sudden, unexpected decision to write a short, vital phrase in English in the context of a letter in French, against the background of so many years of writing to Bussy in French – so many years, their eyes, their ears, their faces so much older now – I think Gide achieves this precious indirection, something that, in the late lectures, Barthes also calls tact. There is a precision to writing an English formula in a French letter – a writing which, in the very moment of its utterance, and in the ongoing present of their correspondence, is made irrepressible, unforeseeable – an exactitude which I think has very precisely to do with its beautifully detoured directness: '*De tout mon coeur bien fatigué*: I love you.'

Dorothy Bussy had ended her letter. She'd concluded, and signed off with her initials. But then the letter takes up and ends again, with the addition of a postscript:

'P.S. One word more – a postscript – the postscript to my life. I do believe those three English words in your letter. I believe, I know, you understand, you mean them. D. B.'

One recent late afternoon, I took the number 85 bus to the Port Royal side of the jardin du Luxembourg. My plan was to walk through the park to the rue Servandoni. To stand for a while in front of the building where Barthes lived and worked for twenty years, from 1960 to 1980, in an apartment on the sixth floor. I had never done so before; over the five or so years of translating the lecture courses, it had never really occurred to me to do so before. But I was thinking, still on that day, of the 'bad mother' glimpsed from the window: the walking woman, hurried, perhaps, and out-of-step – and of the degree to which she might be me.

I walked through the gardens, through the park, past the fountain where the young men gather. Pondering which area of the park might have been wide and open enough for Barthes to play prisoner's base there, as I read he used to with his friends (before he was a young man shyly – or boldly? – chatting literature and philosophy) – when he was still a child. 'What I liked best about that game,' he writes in Richard Howard's translation of this scene, wasn't 'provoking the other team and boldly exposing myself to their right to take me prisoner; what I liked best was to free the prisoners – the effect of which was to put both teams back into circulation: the game started again at zero'. It is the same with language, he suggests: 'in the great game of the powers of speech, we also play prisoner's base: one language only has temporary rights over another; all it takes is for a third language to appear from the ranks for the assailant to be forced to retreat.' Is there something of this order *also* going on in Gide's letter, I wonder? In his small late adjustment to his mode of address, choosing, so suddenly and unexpectedly, to write to Bussy in English, which is to say: in neither his own French nor exactly in her own English, but in something like a third language – effecting a release, starting the game all over again – so late, after so many years – at zero?

I think so. I like to think so. I'd like to think that these rights that one language exerts over another, setting the rules for what can be said, and for who can say it, for what counts as important and what doesn't, are only ever temporary. That all it need take is for a further language to appear – neither the one nor the other, neither aggressor nor retreater, but just different: a different vocabulary, a different rhetoric, a different set of questions and answers – for the power and the positions to be redistributed, and for the game to begin again. I believe in translation's part in this: as a power game between two languages, whose dynamics are, at least in principle, always reversible (writing your French into my English, okay; and now here is my English being written into your French); translation – like literature – as the condition of possibility for a new question, a new set of questions to appear, for a new manner of phrasing or responding to the familiar ones to appear, or indeed for something else, for something apparently or entirely beside the point to appear, for something that I've never thought of, some form of experience that has never happened to me, nor to any one of us playing here, in the rich cities of Europe, in the organized beauty of a Paris public garden, and for that something to release, if only for a moment: to release us and redistribute the power among us, before setting us back into new circulation. (Do translations! Yes, yes, and absolutely.)

I walked through the gates of the park and turned onto the rue Varin, walking on, all the way to the Hotel Aramis, looking for the right turn.

Aramis, Athos, Porthos... I thought: I can't be far now (in *The Three Musketeers* Alexandre Dumas has D'Artagnan lodge at no. 10, rue Servandoni – next door, let's say, to Roland Barthes). But I was: I'd gone too far. When I finally found the street it was empty. Outside no. 11 I stood for a little while in the sun.

I felt that I should probably try imagining a person, a body. Leaning some of his weight against one of the heavy double doors, pushing it open, stepping inside and climbing the stairs marked 'B'.

Or a forefinger punching out the building code: once, twice, several times a day, over the space of twenty years. (Would Barthes's building have had a keypad then as clearly it does now? Or is this me? Imposing my different present, my new temporality?)

I thought of Barthes seated at the writing desk in the apartment on the sixth floor. The small vase of flowers. Daffodils, I think, in the black-and-white photograph I have seen of it. (Although how could that be? The date on the calendar reads Wednesday, 25 August.) The beautiful sixties-style timepiece hanging on a nail; the system of paper arrangement (the high shelf for what is *à faire*, to do; the lower for *attente*); the small bottle of Tipp-ex in the far right-hand corner; a pair of scissors; several small bowls (ashtrays?); a pencil.

But it was hard: imagining the reality of it was hard. The point being, perhaps – or of course (of course, of course) – that I have never been upstairs, *with* Barthes.

I have always been elsewhere: working at the desk by my different window; or outside, like the walking woman, on the street below.

I didn't stay all that long. The summer's afternoon was turning slowly into evening and I'd need to be home soon. The rue Servandoni is an ancient paved street. The pavement outside Barthes's apartment building is fairly wide, but as it inclines up towards the park it narrows to the smallest step. At some point, I thought to myself, the woman glimpsed walking on this stretch of pavement, 'the bad mother' with her empty buggy, her tugged-along son, would have had to walk in the road. It was time to go home. Making my way back to the bus-stop on the edge of the park I found myself walking as one of my kids might: lolloping unevenly up the last stretch of the street, one foot up and the next one down, making a game out of alternating between road and curb. What was I doing? Walking home now, away from Barthes's apartment building, but carrying the work, or a part of it – some parts of it – with me: my own idiosyncratic assimilation, my own problematic appropriation – the line between the two being, as Horton wrote of Helen Lowe-Porter, so danceable and so 'truly thin' – walking a bit awkwardly now, it's true, shifting my weight, but still moving and heading home, the sun warm in my face: what exactly was I – what have I been and what am I still intent on – doing?

Protesting, I think.

By which I mean, in keeping with my sense of Barthes's principle of tact: trying to find ways, in recognition of the common ground that exists between one translator and another, between one translational activity and another, of attending to what is delicate and particular. On my own behalf, clearly: at issue has been *my* translation. The way I think and feel: the books I have thought with and felt with, confronting and being carried by their force. But also in the name of writing translations. In the name of the writers of translations. This little art: the each time uniquely relational, lived-out practice of it.

Yes, that's it: I'm protesting.

Let's say I'm actively parrying against the all-purpose explanation.

Sources

It seemed impossible to me to write an essay about
translation (as a form of close and long-term engagement
with the work of others) without engaging very closely
and at length with the work of others. I have done this
in a variety of ways: citation, translation and citation,
translation and paraphrase, translating and writing into
and out of the passage at hand, writing and speaking with
someone else's words or letting someone else's words write
and speak their way through me. Clearly, the degree to
which any one of those processes is really all that different
from or could be said to *not* involve the others is a central
concern of this book. At one point in *The Neutral*, Barthes
says – in Krauss's and Hollier's translation: 'it is obvious
that knowledge enters the course by means of very
fragmented bits, which can seem offhand... I try to create,
to invent a meaning from independent materials, which I
liberate from their historical, doctrinal "truth" → I take the
referential bits (in fact, bits of reading) and I submit them
to an anamorphosis...' (*The Neutral*, pp. 64-65) I hope in
the notes that follow to indicate some of the ways in which
knowledge, the bits of my reading, have entered this essay,
should readers wish to consult (to read, to retranslate, re-
anamorphosize) the sources themselves.

   The key tutor-text for this book has been Barthes's last
lecture course and a further note of clarification is necessary
here. *La préparation du roman I et II* was first published by
the Editions du Seuil in 2003, under the general direction
of Éric Marty and edited, annotated and introduced by
Nathalie Léger. This volume was a transcription of Barthes's
lecture and seminar notes – the notes he read from (and
adhered very closely to) when delivering the lectures
themselves. My English-language translation was based
on this volume, and published by Columbia University
Press in 2011. The audio recordings were also released
as a CD by Seuil in 2004. In 2016, Seuil published *La*

préparation du roman, cours au Collège de France – this new edition is a transcription, by Nathalie Lacroix, of those audio recordings; in other words, of the performed lectures. When writing this book, I have taken pleasure in working from this later edition, and registering the difference between the notes for the lectures (which have this elliptical, stop-start quality) and the ongoing, unfolding discourse that those notes produced. I have also enjoyed rethinking and reworking my translations – re-engaging with the inexhaustible work of translation – of the notes for certain passages of the course, translating from the more expanded oral version as well as or sometimes instead of the written one. I have indicated what I have been doing, and on the basis of which source, in the notes below.

11   A startling gown of thin, dark silk: the lines in this opening section are taken from Helen Lowe-Porter's 1927 translation of Thomas Mann's *The Magic Mountain* (London: Vintage, 2007), pp. 322–343; in order to condense this scene – which in the novel unfolds over a number of pages – I have slightly modified tense and punctuation.

15   Towards the end of his address he'll speak of Thomas Mann's *The Magic Mountain*: from 'Inaugural Lecture, Collège de France', translated by Richard Howard in Susan Sontag, ed. *Barthes: Selected Writings* (Oxford: Fontana, 1983), p. 477.

17   'Who are my contemporaries?': Roland Barthes, *How to Live Together: Novelistic Simulations of Some Everyday Spaces, Notes for a lecture course and seminar at the Collège de France 1976–1977*, edited by Claude Coste and translated by Kate Briggs (New York: Columbia University Press, 2013), p. 6.

21   Winter is descending: http://ask.metafilter.com/105552/Noubliez-pas-ne-rendre-mon-crayon

22   Like a decalcomania: here I am expanding on Richard Howard's translation of this line from *Roland Barthes by Roland Barthes* which reads: 'Fiction: slight detachment, slight separation which forms a complete, coloured scene, like a decalcomania.' (New York: Hill and Wang, 2010), p. 90.

25   John E. Woods, trans. *The Magic Mountain* (New York: Knopf, 1995). In a *New York Times* review of the new translation, D. J. R. Bruckner, assuming that Lowe-Porter is a 'he', writes: 'All the characters in Thomas Mann's masterpiece *The Magic Mountain* come considerably closer to speaking English in John E. Woods' version than they did in its predecessor, by H. T. Lowe-Porter, first published by Knopf in 1927. Lowe-Porter's apology – "better ... an English version ... done ill than not done at all" – was exaggerated, but his vocabulary was wholly Victorian, and he missed Mann's voice.' *New York Times*, 22 October 1995.

26   The dragon-training book: *How to Train Your Dragon* (London: Hodder, 2010) is Book 1 of Cressida Cowell's 12-book series. Book 3 is titled *How to Speak Dragonese*, but we're not quite there yet...

26   The Apostles speak: Acts 2:5–6.

26   Interview with her translator Ann Goldstein: 'Ann Goldstein on Translating Elena Ferrante and the Inner Workings of the *New*

...   *Yorker*', by Melinda Harvey, *Lithub*, 1 September 2016.

27   'He Stuttered': Gilles Deleuze, *Essays Critical and Clinical*, translated
      by Michael A. Greco and Daniel W. Smith (London: Verso, 1998).
      The essay begins 'It is sometimes said that bad novelists feel the need
      to vary their dialogic markers [*indicatifs*] by substituting for "he said"
      expressions like "he murmured," "he stammered," "he sobbed," "he
      giggled"...', p. 107.

33   A 'little art': in her essay 'On Translating Thomas Mann', Lowe-Porter
      writes of 'the little art of translating'. Her essay is reproduced in full
      in John C. Thirlwall's *In Another Language: A Record of the Thirty-Year
      Relationship between Thomas Mann and His English Translator, Helen
      Tracy Lowe-Porter* (New York: Alfred A. Knopf, 1966).

35   'vegetate intellectually': Thirlwall, *In Another Language*, p. 3. All
      further quotations on this page are taken from Helen Lowe-Porter's
      'On Translating Thomas Mann', pp. 178–209.

36   David Horton, *Thomas Mann in English* (London: Bloomsbury, 2016),
      p. 54.

37   Horton, *Thomas Mann in English*, p. 220.

38   'There is an age': Barthes also describes a third age: from teaching
      what we know, to teaching what we do not know ('this is called
      research') to the 'age of another experience': 'that of *unlearning,* of
      yielding to the unforeseeable change which forgetting imposes on
      the sedimentation of the knowledges, cultures, and beliefs we have
      traversed.' 'Inaugural lecture, Collège de France', p. 478.

38   'research, not a lecture': Barthes, *How to Live Together*, p. 21

41   This is the question that Gérard Genette asks, briefly: in the passage
      I have in mind, Genette is discussing Nelson Goodman's contention
      that what he calls a 'work' should be absolutely identical with its 'text'
      (its 'manifestation'). A translation, of course, is materially different
      from the original – which means that it inevitably fails to meet
      Goodman's criterion of sameness of spelling. Thus, on Goodman's
      terms, each new translation would have to be considered 'a new work'.
      Genette's point is that while this 'simple' position is philosophically
      convenient for a nominalist, it doesn't really fit with the way we
      commonly speak about translations, which authorize us to say,
      indifferently:

...   'I've read a French translation of *War and Peace*', 'I've read *War and Peace* in French', or indeed, in the same situation, and just as easily, 'I've read *War and Peace*.' He writes: 'a likely objection to this would be to say that these locutions follow from a simple metonymy, such as "War and Peace is in the living room"; but it seems to me these two metonymies are not of the same order: the figural slippage from the text to its copy is more sensible (and, as it goes, more 'ontological') than from the text to its translation.' [Editor's note: author's translation.] Gérard Genette, *The Work of Art: Immanence and Transcendence*, translated by G. M. Goshgarian (Cornell: Cornell University Press, 1997), p. 177.

41   'The right words in the right order': what Virginia Woolf wants to stress here is how difficult this is to achieve. 'It is only a matter of finding the right words and putting them in the right order.' 'But,' she goes on, 'we cannot do it because they do not live in dictionaries; they live in the mind. And how do they live in the mind? Variously and strangely...' 'Craftsmanship' in David Bradshaw, ed., *Virginia Woolf: Selected Essays* (Oxford: Oxford University Press, 2008), p. 89.

42   'these specific words in this specific arrangement': Derek Attridge, *The Singularity of Literature* (London and New York: Routledge, 2004), especially p. 75.

45   The performative power of the speech act: Theo Hermans writes: 'the view I am putting forward here is that a translation comes into being when a text that has been written alongside another text is declared to be a translation of that other text. The declaration is an illocutionary speech act ... I regard a translation as initially being merely another text until it is declared to be a translation.' Provided, as he points out, that the speech act succeeds. *The Conference of the Tongues* (London and New York: Routledge, 2007), p. 91.

47   A sort of stammering: Anne Carson, *Nay Rather*, The Cahier Series no. 21 (London: Sylph Editions, 2013), p. 32.

50   There's a moment in Barthes's last lecture course: Roland Barthes, *The Preparation of the Novel, Lecture Courses and Seminars at the Collège de France (1978–1979 and 1979–1980)*, edited by Nathalie Léger and translated by Kate Briggs (New York: Columbia University Press, 2011), p. 207. Here I am retranslating from the transcribed audio recordings of the live delivery of that passage, recently published as *La préparation du roman: Cours au Collège de France 1978–79 et 1979–80*, text annotated by Nathalie Léger, transcription by Nathalie Lacroix (Paris: Seuil, 2016), pp. 380–1.

53 Renee Gladman, poet, novelist and translator, asking her interviewer in an interview: 'Language and Landscape: Renee Gladman' by Zack Freidman, *BOMB Magazine*, 24 December 2011.

53 'loose and evasive appositional syntax': Elizabeth W. Bruss quotes this observation of Culler's in her chapter on Roland Barthes in *Beautiful Theories: The Spectacle of Discourse in Contemporary Criticism* (Baltimore: The Johns Hopkins University Press, 1982), p. 372.

55 the three per cent problem: *The Three Percent Problem: Rants and Responses on Publishing, Translation and the Future of Reading* by Chad W. Post (Open Letter, 2011).

55 Rachel Cooke, 'The subtle art of translating foreign fiction', the *Observer*, 24 July 2016.

58 as Edith Grossman puts it: in *Why Translation Matters* (New Haven and London: Yale University Press, 2010).

60 I'm told that in French the midway scene is this most extraordinary thing: the theorist and translator Antoine Berman discusses the 'heteroglossia' of *Der Zauberberg* in 'Translation and the Trials of the Foreign', translated by Lawrence Venuti, in Venuti, ed., *The Translation Studies Reader,* 2nd edition (New York and London: Routledge, 2005), p. 288.

63 the most 'selfless' art: In a recent interview with the brilliant Spanish to English translator Megan McDowell, McDowell is described as 'the most selfless sort of artist there is'. 'The Making of a Tireless Literary Translator: Why Megan McDowell Never Stops Working', by Nathan Scott McNamara, *Lithub*, 29 March 2017.

65 A lecture, he says, is a specific kind of production: Barthes, *The Preparation of the Novel*, p. 7; here, again, I am translating and paraphrasing from the transcribed audio recordings, *La préparation du roman* (2016), pp. 24–5.

71 'Who we choose to translate is political': Antena is 'a language justice and language experimentation collective' founded in 2010 by Jen Hofer and John Pleuker. The pamphlet titled 'A Manifesto for Ultratranslation' was published by Antena Books/Libros Antena in 2013.

71 we need to vary our choices: 'Translating Poetry, Translating Blackness', by John Keene published on Harriet poetry blog, 2016.

72   'if by some unimaginable excess of socialism or barbarism': Barthes, 'Inaugural Lecture, Collège de France', translated by Richard Howard, pp.462–464.

73   'a very selective, densely motivated choice': Lawrence Venuti, 'Translation, Community, Utopia', in *The Translation Studies Reader*, 2nd edition, p. 488.

74   Lydia Davis's ongoing translation diary: 'Alphabet of Proust Translation Problems' in *Proust, Blanchot and a Woman in Red*, The Cahier Series no. 5 (Lewes: Sylph Editions, 2007), p. 11.

74   Katy Derbyshire researching: Katy Derbyshire, 'Bricks and Mortar by Clemens Meyer –A Translator's Note', http://lovegermanbooks. blogspot.co.uk/2016/10/bricks-and-mortar-by-clemens-meyer.html.

75   In November 1995 the scholar Timothy Buck published an article: I am quoting variously here from the three different published versions of Buck's assessment of Lowe-Porter's translations: 'Neither the letter not the spirit: Why most translations of Thomas Mann are so inadequate', *Times Literary Supplement*, 13 October 1995; the chapter titled 'Mann in English' in *The Cambridge Companion to Thomas Mann*, edited by Ritchie Robertson (Cambridge: Cambridge University Press, 2002) and the Thomas Mann entry in the *Encyclopedia of Literary Translation into English Vol. 2, M-Z*, edited by Olive Classe (London and Chicago: Fitzroy Dearborn Publishers, 2000).

78   In a recent interview in the *Los Angeles Review of Books*, Gayatri Spivak: 'Critical Intimacy: an Interview with Gayatri Chakravorty
…   Spivak' by Steve Paulson, *LA Review of Books*, 29 July 2016.

80   Lady Rothermere: the letter was dated 10 November 1918. *The Selected Letters of André Gide and Dorothy Bussy*, edited and translated by Richard Tedeschi with an introduction by Jean Lambert (Oxford and New York: Oxford University Press, 1983).

80   'little masterpiece': in a letter dated 5 June 1948; *Selected Letters*, p. 284.

82   an accident: for example, in an interview by Liesl Schillinger, Goldstein is asked:'Do you remember when you first became aware of translation as something you might do professionally?' She replies: 'It happened by accident in 1992'. 'Multilingual Wordsmiths, Part 4: Ann Goldstein on "Ferrante Fever"', *Los Angeles Review of Books,* 29 May 2016.

84   a small rush of letters: for further discussion of Buck's article, its
     responses and the questions this case raises for translation and
     Translation Studies more generally, see Theo Hermans's preamble
     to *Translation in Systems* (London and New York: Routledge, 1994)
     titled 'Mann's Fate'. Venuti's letters to the *TLS* were published on 24
     November and 22 December 1995; David Luke's replies on 8 and
     29 December 1995; the letter from Helen Lowe-Porter's daughters,
     Frances Fawcett and Patricia Lowe, was published on 19 January 1996.

85   A perverse pleasure: this line and the ones that follow are taken from
     Buck's original article, with the exception of 'look to the whole' which
     comes from the daughters' letter, reproducing their mother's letter to
     her publisher. The full passage reads: 'Another principle I have, which
     I may just mention, because a lot of people mightn't agree with it, is
     substitution. Each language has its own genius, though some are more
     alike in genesis and growth. I may come on a fine idiomatic or allusive
     phrase in the German and find that the English just doesn't lend itself
     to the same effect. But perhaps another sentence somewhere else in
     the text can display the same kind of literary virtue in English ... But it
     makes the reviewer's job harder. He has to look at the whole, and not
     pick out sentences, if he wishes to judge the translation at all.'

86   In a recent exasperated critical review: Geoffrey Bennington,
     'Embarrassing Ourselves', *Los Angeles Review of Books*, 20 March 2016.

89   'Of course it's good to get things right': Michael Wood, 'Impossible
     Wishes,' *London Review of Books*, 6 February 2003.

89   'Do we write better?': Virginia Woolf, 'Craftsmanship', p. 89.

96   'The coming day had thrust a long arm into the night': Murdoch,
     Under the Net, p. 121.

97   'Everything had a theory, and yet there was no master theory': Iris
     Murdoch, *Under the Net* (London: Vintage, 2002), pp. 65–66. The line
     breaks in the long quotation here are my own.

100 Why write? Why writing?: a section titled 'The Desire to Write:
     origin and departure', *The Preparation of the Novel*, pp. 130–167,
     especially pages 130–32; here, once again, I am basing my translations
     on the recently published transcriptions of the audio recordings, *La
     préparation du roman* (2016), pp. 241–262, especially pages 241–43.

100 'I may have often flirted': *The Preparation of the Novel*, p. 15.

103 passion for typologies: Susan Sontag, 'Writing Itself: On Roland Barthes', *Barthes: Selected Writings*, p. xii–xiii.

103 two types of reader: illustrated, Barthes says, 'by two ancient words, one Latin, the other Greek: *Volupia*, goddess of fully satisfied Desire, of Fulfillment symbol ≠ *Pothos*, poignant desire for the absent thing.' *The Preparation of the Novel*, p. 132.

104 the reading that passes us by: 'We pass most things in novels as we pass things on a train. The words flow by like the scenery. All is change.' William Gass, 'The Concept of Character in Fiction', in Michael J. Hoffman and Patrick D. Murphy, eds. *Essentials of the Theory of Fiction* (Durham and London: Duke University Press, 2005), p. 116.

104 'my Desire to write doesn't stem from reading as such': *The Preparation of the Novel*, p. 132.

104 but *In Search of Lost Time,* not the earlier *Jean Santeuil*: *The Preparation of the Novel*, p. 13.

104 'I dined two or three times at the Governor's house': Marcel Proust, *In Search of Lost Time,* vol. 6: *Times Regained*, translated by Andreas Mayor and Terence Kilmartin, revised by D. J. Enright (London: Chatto and Windus, 1992), p. 284.

105 That's it, says Barthes: in this passage I am translating and paraphrasing the transcribed audio recordings of the lectures, *La préparation du roman*, pp. 243–4. For my translation of the passage in note-form, see *The Preparation of the Novel*, pp. 131–2.

107 'I like': *Roland Barthes by Roland Barthes*, translated by Richard Howard, pp. 116–7; I have slightly revised Howard's translation.

108 how disappointing he found them, how tiresome: Jonathan Culler, 'Preparing the Novel: Spiralling Back', Jürgen Pieters and Kris Pint, *Roland Barthes Retroactively: Reading the Collège de France Lectures, Paragraph*, Vol. 31, No. 1, March 2008, p. 109.

110 'Translators are never': Douglas Robinson, *The Translator's Turn* (Baltimore and London: The Johns Hopkins University Press, 1991), p. 260.

110 'A holistic, gendered, literary being': Michelle Woods, *Kafka Translated: How Translators have Shaped our Reading of Kafka* (London

...   and New York: Bloomsbury, 2014), p. 6.

111   'As for me': *Selected Letters of André Gide and Dorothy Bussy*, p.35.

112   *'J'ai toujours eu envie'*: Barthes, *La Chambre claire: Note sur la
       photographie, Œuvres complètes vol 5*, Éric Marty, ed. (Paris: Seuil,
       2002), p. 791; *Camera Lucida: Reflections on Photography*, translated by
       Richard Howard (New York: Hill and Wang, 2010), p. 18.

114   trying, 'in one's teaching': Lucy O'Meara, 'Some Remarks on Roland
       Barthes's Lectures', *The Conversant*, special issue on the 'Renaissance
       of Roland Barthes' guest edited by Alex Wermer-Colan, 19 August
       2014.

114   a moment in the course on the Neutral: *The Neutral, Lecture Course
       at the Collège de France (1977-1978)*, edited by Thomas Clerc and
       translated by Rosalind E. Krauss and Denis Hollier (New York:
       Columbia University Press, 2005), p. 117.

114   Gilles Deleuze on the interview: Gilles Deleuze and Claire Parnet,
       Dialogues II, translated by Hugh Tomlinson and Barbara Habberjam
       (New York: Columbia University Press, 2007), p. 1.

115   'I' is a *method*: *The Preparation of the Novel*, p. 23.

115   I'd say, Barthes says: here I am translating and worrying over my
       translation of the transcribed audio recordings of this opening
       lecture, especially over how to translate *les leurres*; *La préparation du
       roman* (2016), p. 14.

116   'Every beautiful work': here I am translating from the transcribed
       audio recordings, *La préparation du roman* (2016),p. 245; for the same
       passage in note-form, see *The Preparation of the Novel*, p. 132.

117   Here is life 'in the form of a sentence': *The Preparation of the Novel*,
       p. 97.

117   'Has it never happened': Barthes, 'Reading Writing', *The Rustle of
       Language*, translated by Richard Howard (Berkeley and Los Angeles:
       University of California Press, 1989), p. 29.

119   he makes an inventory of some of them: *The Preparation of the Novel*,
       p. 133.

121 Elena Ferrante has written: all quotations in these pages are taken from Elena Ferrante, 'What an Ugly Child She Is', translated by Ann Goldstein, *The New Yorker*, 31 October 2016.

122 'stylistics of being': See, for example, the section 'Se donner des modèles' in Marielle Macé, *Façons de lire, manières d'être* (Paris: Gallimard, 2011), which discusses at length Barthes's notion of life 'in the form of a sentence'; see too Macé's more recent book, *Styles, critique de nos formes de vie* (Paris: Gallimard, 2016).

122 'formed, fashioned (remote-controlled)': Barthes writes: 'Madame Bovary ... her loves, her dislikes, come from Sentences (see the passage on the books she reads in the convent and what follows), and she dies by the Sentence...' A moment later he says: 'Many – if not all – of us are *Bovarys*: the Sentence directs us...' *The Preparation of the Novel*, p. 99.

125 'I know the novel is dead': Barthes is quoted as saying 'I think of myself not as a critic but as a novelist – not of the novel but of the
... novelistic. I love the novelistic but I know the novel is dead.' In 'Twenty Key Words for Roland Barthes', *The Grain of the Voice, Interviews 1962–1980*, translated by Linda Coverdale (New York: Hill and Wang, 1985), p. 222.

126 a certain constitutional weakness: *The Preparation of the Novel*, p. 15; here I am translating from the transcribed audio recordings, *La préparation du roman* (2016), pp. 43–4.

129 vast, dying sea: Nicholson Baker, *U and I: A True Story* (London: Granta, 2011), p. 15.

131 'For the other's work to pass in me': I am paraphrasing this scene here, lifting some lines directly from Barthes, *The Preparation of the Novel*, p. 134.

135 Barthes cites Julio Cortázar: from *Conversationes con Cortázar* (1978), *The Preparation of the Novel*, p. 280.

135 a more recent interview with Javier Marías: Nicholas Wroe, 'Javier Marías: A Life in Writing,' *The Guardian*, 22 February 2013.

136 the sight of a mother glimpsed from Barthes' window: *How to Live Together*, p. 9.

137   'Translation stops me in my tracks': Jen Hofer, 'Proximate
      Shadowing: Translation as Radical Transparency and Excess,' Poetry
      Foundation, 30 April 2016.

142   Lydia Davis explains: cited in Julian Barnes, 'Writer's Writer and
      Writer's Writer's Writer', *London Review of Books*, 18 November 2010.

144   her recent inventory of the pleasures of translating: Lydia Davis,
      'Eleven Pleasures of Translating', *New York Review of Books*, 8
      December 2016.

146   'the dribble of money': *In Another Language*, p. 21; 'in the intervals of
      rocking the cradle', p. 180; 'ten-year stint', p. 27.

147   'the job is to some extent an artist job': wrote Lowe-Porter in a letter
      to Alfred Knopf, dated 20 December 1947, quoted in Thirlwall, *In
      Another Language*, p. 105.

148   hidden masters of our culture: Maurice Blanchot, 'Translating',
      Friendship, translated by Elizabeth Rottenberg (Stanford: Stanford
      University Press, 1997), p. 57.

151   'It makes me very happy to feel': *Selected Letters of André Gide and
      Dorothy Bussy*, pp. 21–2.

151   'it was with a very keen emotion': *Selected Letters of André Gide and
      Dorothy Bussy*, p. 155; on reading her annotated copy of Tacitus's
      History, pp. 289–90.

152   For Éric Marty: 'Gide et Dorothy Bussy', *André Gide et L'Angleterre,*
      edited by Patrick Pollard (London: Birkbeck College, 1986).

152   will be loved back: on this, I recently read Brian Dillon quoting from
      Maggie Nelson's *Bluets*: 'And what kind of madness is it anyway to
      be in love with something constitutionally incapable of loving you
      back? Are you sure – one would like to ask – that it cannot love you
      back?', *Essayism* (London: Fitzcarraldo Editions, 2017), p. 40.

153   Which is all well and good: Peter Cole, 'Making Sense in Translation:
      Towards an Ethics of the Art', *In Translation: Translators on Their
      Work and What it Means*, edited by Susan Bernofsky and Esther Allen
      (New York: Columbia University Press, 2013), p. 7.

153   'I cannot enter into the work of other writers': Thirlwall, *In Another
      Language*, p. 21.

153 'For thirty-five years I have had a secondary but constant side job': Anita Raja, 'Translation as a Practice of Acceptance', translated by Rebecca Falkoff and Stiliana Milkova, *Asymptote*, 2016.

156 I don't like translations: here I am translating and paraphrasing lines from the transcribed audio recordings, *La préparation du roman* (2016), p. 528.

156 Richard Howard narrates an early incident: 'Editor and Author: Marion Duvert and Richard Howard on Barthes', *FSG Work-in-Progress*, October 2010.

157 'As a general rule, translations present a very serious obstacle to my reading': here I am translating from the transcribed audio recordings, *La préparation du roman* (2016), pp. 63–4; see also, *The Preparation of the Novel*, pp. 24–5.

158 'Why is it that I have such little taste for foreign languages?': *Roland Barthes by Roland Barthes*, translated by Richard Howard, p. 115.

159 'constant summonings': Nicholson Baker, *U and I: A True Story*, p. 30.

160 new ways of thinking relationality on a micro-scale: Adrienne Ghaly, 'Cultural Theory on a Micro-Scale: Roland Barthes's lectures at the Collège de France', *What's so Great about Roland Barthes?* Special Issue of *L'Esprit créateur*, guest edited by Thomas Baldwin, Katja Haustein and Lucy O'Meara, Vol. 55, No. 4, Winter 2015, pp. 39–55.

162 'Again, after overcast days': 'Deliberation', translated by Richard Howard, in *Barthes: Selected Writings*, pp. 484–5.

162 'If I were a haiku-writer': I am translating and quoting here from the transcribed audio recordings, *La préparation du roman* (2016), pp. 111–2.

163 'Roland Barthes and Poetry': *Barthes Studies Vol. 2: Roland Barthes and Poetry*, guest edited by Calum Gardner, 26 November 2016.

163 Like a leaf falling: in *Roland Barthes by Roland Barthes*, Barthes describes a project for a book called *Incidents* '(mini-texts, one-liners, haiku, notations, puns, everything that falls, like a leaf, etc.)', translated by Richard Howard, p. 150.

165 one must never underestimate the layout of a haiku: see the section

...   titled 'Typography. Aeration' in *The Preparation of the Novel*, p.
      26. The hand-out or 'fascicule' is reproduced in *La préparation du
      roman I et II, Cours et séminaires au Collège de France (1978–1979 et
      1979–1980)*, edited by Nathalie Léger (Paris Seuil / IMEC, 2003),
      pp. 461–63.

166   It's very important to me but: here I am translating and paraphrasing
      on the basis of the transcribed audio recordings, *La préparation du
      roman* (2016), p. 72.

167   Spring, Summer-Autumn, and Autumn-Winter: *Haiku,* 4 vols.,
      edited and translated by R.H. Blyth (Tokyo: The Hokuseido Press,
      1949–1952).

169   'discreet but discernible gay specificity': D. A. Miller, *Bringing Out
      Roland Barthes* (Berkeley, Los Angeles and Oxford: University of
      California Press, 1992), p. 16.

169   erotics of proximity and distance: *How to Live Together*, pp. 72–75.

169   the fantasy of the dressmaker: *The Preparation of the Novel*, p. 22.

176   let pass apparently untouched: on the untranslated status of proper
      names see Jacques Derrida, 'from Des Tours de Babel', translated
      by Joseph G. Graham, *Theories of Translation: An Anthology of Essays
      from Dryden to Derrida*, edited by Rainer Schulte and John Biguenet
      (Chicago and London: The University of Chicago Press, 1992), pp.
      218–227.

178   'One Always Fails in Speaking of What One Loves': translated by
      Richard Howard in *The Rustle of Language*, pp. 296–305.

179   'Attention! when I speak of these writer-heroes': 'Take note: the
      great writer isn't someone you can compare yourself to but someone
      whom you can, whom you want to, identify with, to a greater or
      less extent.' *The Preparation of the Novel*, p. 3 (although the refrain is
      repeated a number of times throughout the course: see, for example,
      p. 129).

181   'It's not true that the more you love': *A Lover's Discourse: Fragments*,
      translated by Richard Howard (New York: Hill and Wang, 2001),
      p. 135.

182   'When you are translating, you are working in partnership': Lydia
      Davis, 'Eleven Pleasures of Translating'.

183 Barthes announces the good news: here I am translating and paraphrasing from the transcribed audio recordings, *La préparation du roman*, p. 74.

187 Blyth, after all, 'was a brilliant translator': Adrian James Pinnington, 'Haiku in English Translation', *Encyclopedia of Literary Translation into English: Vol. 1, A–L*, edited by Olive Classe (London and Chicago: Fitzroy Dearborn Publishers, 2000), pp. 604–6.

188 'A UK view of Pinks vs. Carnations': Caroline Whetman, 'A UK View of Pinks vs. Carnations', *The Flower Expert*, 13 July 2006.

188 Like the physicists: *The Preparation of the Novel*, p. 75.

189 *stoppeuse*: here I am translating and paraphrasing from the transcribed audio recordings, *La préparation du roman*, pp. 464–65.

195 '*amator*: one who loves and loves again': *Roland Barthes by Roland Barthes*, translated by Richard Howard, p. 52.

197 'passages whose meaning I understood perfectly': Simon Leys, *Notes from the Hall of Uselessness*, translated by Dan Gunn, The Cahier Series no. 9 (Lewes: Sylph Editons, 2008), p. 27.

198 'Translation as Scholarship': Catherine Porter, 'Translation as Scholarship', *In Translation: Translators on Their Work and What it Means*, pp. 58–66.

200 'how much we need to know': the essay is also a review of Alex Beam's *The Feud: Vladimir Nabokov, Edmund Wilson and the End of a Beautiful Friendship* (Pantheon, 2016), Caryl Emerson, 'Word Wars', *The Chronicle of Higher Education*, 29 January 2017.

201 'It is a pleasure': *Selected Letters of André Gide and Dorothy Bussy,* pp. 141–2. Line breaks are my own.

205 Lydia Davis had recently published some of her own translations: we have been working on A. L. Snijders's *De Mol en andere dierenzkv's* (AFdH Uitgevers, 2009); Davis's translations have been published in *Asymptote* and *The White Review*.

207 The idea of the unschooled: see Jacques Rancière, *The Ignorant Schoolmaster: Five Lessons in Intellectual Emancipation*, translated by Kristin Ross (Stanford: Stanford University Press, 1991).

210 'If you are interested in talking about the other': Gayatri Spivak, 'The Politics of Translation' in Lawrence Venuti, ed., *The Translation Studies Reader,* 2nd edition (New York and London: Routledge, 2004), p. 407.

213 'The middle-class maiden': *Roland Barthes by Roland Barthes,* translated by Richard Howard, p. 52.

215 as Adrien Chassain argues: Adrien Chassain, 'Roland Barthes: « Les pratiques et valeurs de l'amateur »' *Fabula,* 1 October 2015.

216 a lesson plan for children: 'Literature / Teaching', *The Grain of the Voice,* translated slightly modified after Linda Coverdale, pp. 233–42.

218 'A society is beautiful': 'Concert de musique de chambre par trois étudiants de Belledonne', *Existences,* 1945, republished in *Roland Barthes, Oeuvres complètes, 5 volumes* (Paris: Seuil, 2001), vol. 1, p. 83. quoted by Chassain.

219 the way our reading informs our living: see Marielle Macé, *Façons de lire, manières d'être* (Paris: Gallimard, 2011).

224 some fifteen hundred: Gustave Flaubert, *Bouvard and Pécuchet,* translated by Mark Polizzotti (Dallas: Dalkey Archive Press, 2005), p. vii.

227 idiorrhythmy: see the section titled 'My Fantasy: Idiorrhythmy' in *How to Live Together,* pp. 6–9.

230 *Living with the Tudors*: *Living with the Tudors* (UK, 2007), a film by Karen Guthrie and Nina Pope.

232 'a dismal book': George Orwell, 'Charles Reade', *The Collected Non-Fiction,* edited by Peter Davison (London: Penguin, 2017), p. 671.

233 an oddly *event-less* novel: *How to Live Together,* p. 84.

234 'And here I must needs observe': Daniel Defoe, *Robinson Crusoe* (Ware: Wordsworth Classics, 1995) pp. 51–2

236 'Labours of Love': Boyd Tonkin, 'Labours of Love: Literary Translation Inside and Outside the Marketplace', Taylor and Francis Online, 24 February 2017.

237   produces only for use, not for exchange: See Stephen Hymer, 'Robinson Crusoe and the Secret of Primitive Accumulation', *Monthly Review*, Vol. 63, Issue 4 (September), 2011 (a reprint of an article which first appeared in 1971).

237   A proxemical object: *How to Live Together*, p. 111.

237   no problem making rectangles: *How to Live Together*, p. 114–16.

237   wheel in the wheelbarrow: for a fascinating discussion of circles and the effort to re-invent the wheel in Robinson Crusoe see Jacques Derrida, *The Beast and the Sovereign vol. 1*, translated by Geoffrey Bennington (Chicago: University of Chicago Press, 2009).

238   projectile: *The Preparation of the Novel*, p. 149.

241   'I wish more novelists translated novels': Chad W. Post, 'Interview with Adam Thirlwell', *Three Percent*, 24 July 2008,

242   'Glory, for the translator': Tim Parks, 'The Translation Paradox', *NYRB Daily*, 15 March 2016.

244   'the catalogue of their shared tastes': *A Lover's Discourse: Fragments*, translated by Richard Howard, p. 199.

250   de- and re-contextualisation: Lawrence Venuti, *Translation Changes Everything: Theory and Practice* (London and New York: Routledge, 2013). Venuti makes this point repeatedly throughout his work but see, for example, p. 180.

252   'As a temporary or permanent substitute for creation': Simon Leys, *Notes from the Hall of Uselessness*, translated by Dan Gunn, p. 30.

254   'with just a slight hesitation': Dan Gunn, 'The Lydia Davis Interview', *The Quarterly Conversation*, 10 March 2014.

257   'One of the ways to get around the confines of one's "identity"': Gayatri Spivak, 'The Politics of Translation', p. 369.

258   'which scraggly oak leaf': Maggie Nelson, *The Argonauts* (Minneapolis, Minnesota: Graywolf Press, 2015), pp. 20–21.

261   *The Nature and Art of Workmanship*: David Pye, *The Nature and Art of Workmanship* (London: The Herbert Press, 1995), pp. 20–29.

263 'Here am I working eight hours a day in an insurance office': George Orwell, *The Road to Wigan Pier* (London: Secker and Warburg, 1997), p. 186.

266 'Gotcha!': Michelle Woods, *Kafka Translated: How Translators have Shaped Our Readings of Kafka*, p. 85.

267 'soundness' and 'comeliness': Pye, *The Nature and Art of Workmanship*, pp. 30–31.

269 practical writing matters: *The Preparation of the Novel*, pp. 20–22; here I am also translating and paraphrasing from the transcribed audio recordings, *La préparation du roman*, pp. 55–56.

271 '*Longtemps je me suis couché de bonne heure*': here I am slightly modifying and writing into Richard Howard's translation, '*Longtemps je me suis couché de bonne heure*', *The Rustle of Language*, pp. 277–78.

272 a domestic working practice: *The Preparation of the Novel*, p. 22.

273 '"thin" or minimalist relations to the world': Adrienne Ghaly, 'Cultural Theory on a Micro-Scale: Roland Barthes's Lectures at the Collège de France', pp. 47–8.

274 There's an essay by Paul Valéry: 'Variations on the *Eclogues*', translated by Denise Folliot, *Theories of Translation: An Anthology of Essays from Dryden to Derrida*, edited by Rainer Schulte and John Biguenet (Chicago and London: The University of Chicago Press, 1992), pp. 113–126.

278 I hardly knew any Latin: all these lines are lifted from Denise Folliot's translation of Valéry's essay (the line breaks are my own).

280 what Anita Raja in her lecture: Anita Raja, 'Translation as a Practice of Acceptance'.

282 by a guy whom Barthes once sat next to on a bus: in fact, it was almost every line, not every single line. But my misremembering speaks to the point I want to make about translation, I think, which is that the translator must indeed reproduce every single line of the work-to-be-translated. See *The Preparation of the Novel*, p. 191.

283 Abbé Prévost's French version of *Pamela*: see Lawrence Venuti, 'Translation, Community, Utopia', *The Translation Studies Reader*,

...   2nd edition, edited by Lawrence Venuti (London and New York: Routledge, 2005), p. 484; H. M. Parshley's translation of *The Second Sex* was first published in 1953; the book was recently retranslated in full by Constance Borde and Sheila Malovany-Chevallier (London: Cape, 2009); Paul Legault, *The Emily Dickinson Reader* (San Francisco: McSweeney's, 2012).

285   the point that Jacques Derrida makes: Jacques Derrida, 'What is a Relevant Translation?' translated by Lawrence Venuti, *The Translation Studies Reader*, 2nd edition, p. 427.

285   'footnotes rising up the page like skyscrapers': Vladimir Nabokov, 'Problems of Translation: Onegin in English', *The Translation Studies Reader*, 2nd edition, p. 83.

285   'one seventh': David Damrosch, 'Translation and World Literature: Love in the Necropolis', Lawrence Venuti, ed. *The Translation Studies Reader,* 3rd ed. (London and New York: Routledge, 2012), p. 419.

285   'a certain approximation of form': Valéry, 'Variations on the *Eclogues*', p. 120.

289   There's a panel discussion you can watch on YouTube: 'Translating Kafka', *London Review of Books* event, 2012.

291   'When I had wrought out some boards': Defoe, *Robinson Crusoe*, p. 52.

293   Philosophy, observes Sara Ahmed, is full of tables: Sara Ahmed, *Queer Phenomenology: Orientations, Objects, Others* (Durham and London: Duke University Press, 2006), p. 3.

293   Marx, too: Karl Marx, *Capital: A Critique of Political Economy*, vol 1., trans. Ben Fowkes (New York: Vintage, 1977), p. 163fn.

293   'all the tables': Jacques Derrida, *Specters of Marx: The State of Debt, the Work of Mourning and the New International*, translated by Peggy Kamuf (New York and London: Routledge, 2006), p. 190.

294   'Think of a kitchen table ... when you're not there': Virginia Woolf, *To the Lighthouse* (Wordsworth Editions, 2002), p. 17.

296   the way Oana Avasilichioaei and Erín Moure run the word 'translation': 'Anatomy of a Temperature' (from *Expeditions of a Chimaera*), excerpted in *I'll Drown My Book: Conceptual Writing by*

...   *Women*, edited by Caroline Bergvall et al (Los Angeles: Les Figues Press, 2012), pp. 32–33.

305   one of the reasons given for publishing the course again: see Bernard Comment, 'Avant-propos', *La préparation du roman* (2016), p. 10.

306   'What work goes into the making of things': Sara Ahmed, *Queer Phenomenology*, p. 40.

307   some of the pioneering work of Translation Studies: see Jean-Paul Vinay and Jean Darbelnet's 'A Methodology for Translation', in *The Translation Studies Reader,* 2nd edition, pp. 128–137; Susan Bernofsky, 'Translation and the Art of Revision', *In Translation: Translators on Their Work and What it Means*, pp. 223–33; Jacqueline Guillemin-Flescher, *Syntaxe comparée du français et de l'anglais: problèmes de traduction* (Paris: Editions Ophrys, 1981).

311   everybody laughed: Horton, *Thomas Mann in English*, p. 68.

312   'Each time that in my pleasure, my desire': *The Neutral*, translated by Rosalind E. Krauss and Denis Hollier, p. 36.

314   translation can make authorial ownership nervous: Emily Apter, 'What is Yours, Ours and Mine: On the Limits of Ownership and the Creative Commons', *October* 126, Fall 2008, pp. 91–114.

318   'It lodged now in the fork of a pear tree': Virginia Woolf, *To the Lighthouse*, p. 17.

322   Clearly, observes David Horton, 'Lowe-Porter felt empowered to intervene': citations here are from Horton's *Thomas Mann in English*; see also Theo Hermans's discussion which opens *Translation in Systems*.

324   A decisive principle of the oeuvre: I am translating here the entry titled 'Délicatesse' in Tiphaine Samoyault's 'Lexique', in *Roland Barthes: L'inattendu, Le Monde Hors-Série*, No. 26, June 2015, p. 113.

325   they acquire their meanings relationally: Ferdinand de Saussure, *Course in General Linguistics*, translated by Roy Harris (London and New York: Bloomsbury, 2013), see for instance, p. 25.

326   'domestic inscription': Lawrence Venuti, 'Translation, Community, Utopia', *The Translation Studies Reader*, p. 485.

327 'A fine responsiveness to the concrete': Martha C. Nussbaum, *Love's Knowledge: Essays on Philosophy and Literature* (Oxford: Oxford University Press, 1990), p. 39, but see also the whole section titled 'The Priority of the Perceptions (Priority of the Particular)', pp. 37–40.

327 Dutch housewife: *The Neutral*, translated by Rosalind E. Krauss and Denis Hollier, p. 30.

328 for as long as I can oppose it to trivial: I have in mind here a line from Rivka Galchen's *Little Labors* (New York: New Directions, 2016) where she writes of the '"small" as opposed to the "minor."'

328 'a special attendant was detailed to wait upon each flower': see *The Neutral*, translated by Rosalind E. Krauss and Denis Hollier, p. 31.

330 'And now I am going to say something very serious': *Selected Letters of André Gide and Dorothy Bussy*, pp. 248–50.

331 'debased' and 'a continuing scandal': cited in Theo Hermans, 'Preamble: Mann's Fate', *Translation in Systems: Descriptive and System-orientated Approaches Explained*, p. 3.

332 tact is *scared*, it is hurt by repetition: *The Neutral*, translated by Rosalind E. Krauss and Denis Hollier, p. 36.

331 'I know you so well and so secretly': *Selected Letters of André Gide and Dorothy Bussy*, p. 133.

333 'I did it because there is a residue': *The Neutral*, translated by Rosalind E. Krauss and Denis Hollier, p. 32.

335 'I am to see Madame Knopf this afternoon at 4': *Selected Letters of André Gide and Dorothy Bussy*, p. 130.

335 D. B.'s translations were poor: *Selected Letters of André Gide and Dorothy Bussy*, p. 130.

336 the fontaine Médicis where the young lycéens would gather: André Gide, *Les Faux-monnayeurs* (Paris: Gallimard, 1925).

338 'a sore point in [her] professional career': *Selected Letters of André Gide and Dorothy Bussy*, p. 177.

339 '"What I should like,"' said Lucien: *The Counterfeiters,* translated by Dorothy Bussy (London: Penguin, 1966), pp. 15–16.

340 Claude Coste calls her 'the bad mother': *How to Live Together,* p. xviii.

341 A translation should be redone every twenty-five years: *The Preparation of the Novel,* p . 23.

341 Elisabeth W. Bruss shows how the timings of those translations imposed a new rhythm of reading and reception: all of the citations in this section come from the chapter titled 'Roland Barthes' in Bruss's *Beautiful Theories: The Spectacle of Discourse in Contemporary Criticism,* pp. 362–461.

344 'How does one organize one's sense of being in the world?': Lucy O'Meara, *Roland Barthes at the Collège de France* (Liverpool: Liverpool University Press, 2012), p. 202; Adrienne Ghaly also cites these lines in her 'Cultural Theory on a Micro-Scale: Roland Barthes's Lectures at the Collège de France', p. 47.

347 The love letter is 'a special dialectic': *A Lover's Discourse: Fragments,* p. 157.

347 'Allow me to write in French': *Selected Letters of André Gide and Dorothy Bussy,* p. 5.

347 Jean Lambert expresses regret: Jean Lambert, ed. *Correspondance André Gide–Dorothy Bussy* (Paris: Gallimard, 1979, 1981, 1982).

349 'My dear Friend,' Bussy writes to Gide: *Selected Letters of André Gide and Dorothy Bussy,* p. 4; p. 116.

351 'It is no use telling you that I am growing very old now': *Selected Letters of André Gide and Dorothy Bussy,* p. 231. The epilogue to the *Selected Letters* reproduces a page: *Selected Letters of André Gide and Dorothy Bussy,* pp. 306–7.

352 '*De tout mon cœur bien fatigué*': *Selected Letters of André Gide and Dorothy Bussy,* p. 286.

353 'Like desire, the love letter waits for an answer': *A Lover's Discourse: Fragments,* translated by Richard Howard, p. 149.

354 *'Je-t'-aime'* / 'I-love-you': *A Lover's Discourse: Fragments*, translated by Richard Howard, p. 158.

355 Bussy's reply to Gide is dated six days later: *Selected Letters of André Gide and Dorothy Bussy*, pp. 286–7.

356 In the preface to his *Critical Essays: Critical Essays*, translated by Richard Howard (Evanston, III.: Northwestern University Press, 1972), p. xiv.

358 'P.S. One word more': *Selected Letters of André Gide and Dorothy Bussy*, p. 287.

360 'What I liked best about that game': *Roland Barthes by Roland Barthes*, translated by Richard Howard, p. 50.

363 in the black-and-white photograph I have seen of it: in *Roland Barthes: L'inattendu, Le Monde Hors-Série*, No. 26, June 2015.

Acknowledgements

Early versions of some passages of this book appeared
first in *The White Review*, *Translation Studies* and *L'Esprit
créateur*. Many thanks to the editors of those publications.

There are a number of people whose work, conversation, generosity and support have directly or indirectly
informed the writing of *This Little Art*. Thank you to Céline
Surprenant, Laura Marcus, Derek Attridge, Nicholas Royle,
Diana Knight, Nathalie Léger, Jennifer Crewe and Ron
Harris of Columbia University Press, Bryan Eccleshall
(for David Pye), Chris Pearson and Patrick Wildgust of
Shandy Hall, Nina Wakeford and Raphaël Zarka. Thank
you to the translators with whom it was my great privilege
and pleasure to translate in the context of a workshop titled
'Translation as Experimentation' (which ran as part of
the Masters in Cultural Translation, directed by Geoffrey
Gilbert of the American University of Paris, between 2011
and 2015). Thank you also to the artists with whom it is
such a privilege and pleasure to write (and to get energized
and emboldened by) on the Masters in Fine Art at the Piet
Zwart Institute, Rotterdam. Thank you to my colleagues in
both institutions, especially Dan Gunn and Daniel Medin
of AUP for the Cahier Series, Vivian Rehberg, Petra van der
Kooij and Steve Rushton (my Calvino-reading friend) of
the Piet Zwart Institute. Special thanks to Niels Bekkema,
Madison Bycroft, Ash Kilmartin and Katherine McBride
who together form our Dutch-English literary translation
group. I am very grateful to Daisy Hildyard, Lucy O'Meara
and Moosje Moti Goosen who read and commented on the
manuscript at different stages of completion, and to Jacques
Testard for freedom, reassurance, editing and everything
else. There are four close friends and readers whose
company in life and whose long-term engagement with this
project neither I nor this book could have done without:
thank you Daniela Cascella, Geoffrey Gilbert, Anna-Louise

Milne and Natasha Soobramanien. Thank you to my Mum and Dad and to Chloe, Tom and Jackson. Finally, thank you to someone whose presence is barely felt in these pages but who has accompanied them and me throughout: Anthony, I dedicate this book to you – and to our sons Arthur and Sam.

Fitzcarraldo Editions
8-12 Creekside
London, SE8 3DX
Great Britain

ISBN 978-1-91069-545-6

Design by Ray O'Meara
Typeset in Fitzcarraldo
Printed and bound by Bell & Bain Ltd, Glasgow

fitzcarraldoeditions.com

Fitzcarraldo Editions